D0847791

Glasshouses and Wintergardens
of the Nineteenth Century

Glasshouses and Wintergardens of the Nineteenth Century

Stefan Koppelkamm

Translated by
Kathrine Talbot

RIZZOLI
NEW YORK

First published in the United States of America
in 1981 by
Rizzoli International Publications, Inc.
712 Fifth Avenue, New York, N. Y. 10019

© Copyright 1981 by Verlag Gerd Hatje, Stuttgart

LC 81-51102
ISBN 0-8478-0387-2

Printed and bound in Western Germany

'It [the greenhouse] is entirely a work of art: the plants enclosed are in the most artificial situation in which they can be placed. . .'

The Greenhouse Companion, London, 1824[1]

I wish to thank those who have helped me in carrying out this project by supplying me with important advice and information, and by looking through the manuscript with me. My special thanks to Daniel Koppelkamm, Heinz Nickel, Manfred and Doris Hegger, Hans Brinkmann, Walter Tiegel, Jörg Katz, Floris M. Neusüss, Simone Fitzau and Harvey Sussock, Jane Low and Peter Byrne, Hage Merz, Eric W. Curtis, Douglas Mackenzie, Michael Pearman, H. J. Buckley, B. R. P. Playle, Susanne Steckbeck, Christian Mackensen, Eva Bovenzi, Axel Menges, Alfred B. Gottwaldt, Thomas Herzog as well as the staff of the British Library and the libraries of the University of California at Berkeley and Stanford, of the Berlin University of Technology and the Kassel comprehensive University.

A research grant from the Kassel comprehensive University enabled me to undertake my first journey in connection with the book.

Contents

The jacket illustration shows
The Royal Glasshouses, Laeken, Belgium

Preface

The origin of my interest in the architecture of glasshouses was not in the first place a scientific one. I was fascinated by the juxtaposition of growing and man-made forms, and by the idea of enclosing nature in a glass case to create an artificial paradise.

This longing for an earthly paradise has shown itself again today, with wintergardens once more to be found in modern architecture. An example which has become a modern classic is the building for the Ford Foundation in New York City, constructed in 1968 and designed by the architects Kevin Roche, John Dinkeloo & Associates. Here a courtyard, cut out of the corner of the site, is enclosed in glass on two sides to the full height of the building, sheltering this 'outdoor space' from the street and protecting the small park from the rigours of the weather. A later building by the same architects, the office building of John Deere in Columbus, Indiana, contains a proper miniature landscape under a glass roof in its inner courtyard.[2]

In Europe, the project by the Viennese architects Haus-Rucker-Co. at the Documenta 5 Exhibition in Kassel gives a contemporary interpretation to the glasshouse theme.

The early examples of glasshouses in this book impress us chiefly by their consistent functionalism. They show that the connection between function and beauty was recognised as far back as the beginning of the nineteenth century, though 'functionalism' as a consistent movement with a definite programme, which was to gain such considerable influence, did not appear until the twentieth century. In the nineteenth century functional buildings were considered merely utilitarian and not thought of as architecture. Though buildings like Joseph Paxton's Crystal Palace of 1851 made a great impression internationally, this was less because of their functional beauty which appeals to us today, than because of their technical virtuosity. Conventional buildings were, on the other hand, expected to use orthodox architectural styles and traditional materials.

One of the most important innovators in the design of glasshouses was the Scotsman John Claudius Loudon, who was both an architect and one of the most productive horticultural and architectural writers of the nineteenth century. Both his writings and his experimental glasshouses were far in advance of his time:

'Indeed, there is hardly any limit to the extent to which this sort of light roof might not be carried: several acres, even a whole country residence, where the extent was moderate, might be covered in this way, by the use of hollow cast-iron columns as props, which might serve also as conduits for the water which fell on the roof. Internal showers might be produced in Loddiges' manner; or the roof might be of the polyprosopic kind, and opened at pleasure to admit the natural rain. Any required temperature might be kept up by the use of concealed tubes of steam, and regulated by the apparatus of Kewley. Ventilation also would be effected by the same machine. The plan of such a roof might either be flat ridges running north and south or octagon or hexagon cones, with a supporting column at each angle, raised to the height of a hundred or a hundred and fifty feet from the ground, to admit of the tallest oriental trees, and the undisturbed flight of appropriate birds among their branches. A variety of oriental birds and monkeys, and other animals, might be introduced; and in ponds, a stream made to run by machinery, and also in salt lakes, – fishes, polypo, corals, and other productions of fresh or sea-water might be cultivated or kept.

'The great majority of readers will no doubt consider these ideas as sufficiently extravagant; but there is no limit to human improvement, and few things afford a greater proof of it than the comforts and luxuries man receives from the use of glass. . .'[3]

It was the pioneering spirit of men such as Paxton and Loudon which helped create many of the glasshouses shown in this book and to push forward the boundaries of nineteenth century construction and design.

'Oasis No. 7', Kassel (1972), Haus-Rucker-Co.

Definitions

'Planthouses, also called glasshouses, are designed to protect plants which grow in warmer regions from harsher climates, and to make it possible to grow indigenous plants in the cold season.'[4]

The function of the glasshouse could not be described more succinctly. If we look at the appropriate chapter in John Claudius Loudon's *Encyclopaedia of Gardening*, we find first of all a distinction between movable, temporary structures, and permanent, fixed buildings.

The first group comprises, among others, glass-covered wooden forcing frames for covering beds, and frames which can be put up along a wall over single trees or bushes. It is mainly the second group of 'permanent'[5] buildings that will be our concern in this book, as we shall leave aside structures used predominantly for commercial crops which were similar to those still in use today.

Permanent planthouses can be divided into the following types.

(1) The Orangery

The orangery was the planthouse of the eighteenth century and was used to house oranges, pomegranates, myrtles, etc. through the winter months. Its most important function was to keep the temperature around the plants above freezing. The orangery, which often stood within the precincts of a castle, was designed to be in tune with the living quarters and ornamental buildings around it. A structure of brick or stone, it had large divided windows facing south, and a solid roof.

(2) Structures which form the transition from the orangery to the large planthouse of glass and iron.

These buildings resemble the orangery in their groundplan and appearance but have glass roofs, with a glass dome rather than a flat roof over the central part of the building. This type of building was first used in the early nineteenth century.

(3) The Greenhouse

Also known as plant- or forcing house, this building is used to grow and propagate decorative and useful plants. These simple, purpose-built structures, much as we still find them in many nurseries, usually have a back wall to the north, and a sloping glass roof facing south leaning against this wall. These greenhouses have a relatively narrow cross-section, but are often very long.

The plants stand in pots on tables or on pedestals rising like steps towards the back wall or, when the building faces east and west, they rise towards the centre.

(4) The Glasshouse or Conservatory

Here the plants do not grow in pots but in the earth. This type of planthouse is used mainly for collecting plants of botanical interest or for scientific purposes. Since tall exotic plants like bamboos, tree ferns or palms are often grown here, the buildings are correspondingly taller.

In botanical gardens many varieties of plants were often grown together, the higher central part being used for palms. The rectangular shape of these buildings, which were divided into several sections, was derived from the groundplan of the orangery. Most of them were constructed of iron and glass, letting in the light from all sides.

(5) The Wintergarden or Conservatory

These names refer more to the use made of the buildings than their type, for orangeries, as well as buildings in categories (2) and (4), could be used as wintergardens. Small glasshouses which were partly or wholly used as wintergardens or conservatories were often attached to a house.

These buildings, described in the *Handbook of Architecture* as 'ornamental and show buildings',[6] were mainly used to add to the living space of a house or apartment. Horticultural or scientific considerations were secondary. But as well as private, there are also public wintergardens and conservatories.

Other distinctions can be made according to various climatic conditions, or to the type of plant kept in the building. Thus we have cold houses, hot (tropical) houses, as well as temperate houses. There are also a whole series of special buildings for a variety of plants, such as fern and palm houses, camellia houses, houses for water plants, etc. The type of plant itself dictates the climate and character of the building.

Where, as in the wintergardens, the welfare of the plants is not of primary importance, the temperature is adapted to the convenience of the people who use it, and this in turn governs the choice of plants.

(6) The Winterpalace

The winterpalace is a development of the public wintergarden. Winterpalaces are multi-purpose buildings which appeared in many European cities in the 1870s. Within these buildings the wintergarden itself is only a part of a larger area devoted to leisure activities.

The photographic documentation of buildings which are still standing today is confined to those types of structure first built in the nineteenth century as the result of the new building materials and new methods of construction of the time, such as the transitional forms between the orangery and large greenhouses of iron and glass (2), glasshouses of iron and glass (4), and wintergardens (5).

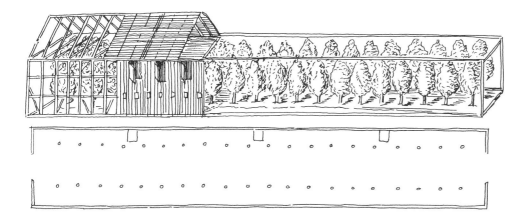

Portable orange house in the Schlossgarden, Heidelberg (before 1620).

Origins

Attempts to raise and keep plants in specially created structures independent of climate and seasons go back to antiquity. Remains of greenhouses found in Pompeii were probably covered in thin panes of translucent stone, but medium size glass panes were already produced there as early as the second century BC by a process of casting.

The history of the modern glasshouse begins in the Renaissance. The voyages of discovery of the fifteenth century launched both colonisation and world trade. Trading companies were founded for this purpose, and they took over the exploitation of the Spanish-Portuguese and British colonial empires. A flood of new products came on to the European market. Exotic fruits, unknown until then, became popular with the princes and rich merchants of Europe. But the merchant ships also brought new plants, seeds and flower bulbs, providing the newly created botanical gardens as well as the wealthy plant collectors with a constant supply of new material.

By the eighteenth century geographical discoveries were largely at an end, but botanical exploration continued well into the nineteenth century.

The most important new fruits were oranges which were said to have first reached Europe towards the end of the thirteenth century. By the end of the fifteenth century, orange trees were grown in Europe. The Italian courts in particular took a great deal of trouble raising citrus fruit, and orange trees soon became popular and spread from there to other European countries where they became part of courtly life by the middle of the sixteenth century. Its rarity gave the orange great prestige. In Van Eyck's portrait of *Giovanni Arnolfini and his Bride* (1434) the oranges on the window ledge in the background are a discreet indication of the high living standard of the couple.

But during the cold season the orange trees had to be protected. When the trees were planted direct in the earth they had somehow to be covered. When they grew in wooden tubs they could be moved into a building. Existing structures, like garden rooms, grottos or open galleries which could be closed with wooden shutters in winter, were often used. But soon buildings began to be produced which were designed specifically for this purpose.

It was at the German courts of Stuttgart, Heidelberg and Munich that the first temporary buildings designed to be dismantled in the summer and re-erected during the winter months over orange grees 'growing in the ground' were first known.

In Stuttgart, where there was already a fig house as far back as 1609, a mobile orange house on rollers, to be pushed over the orange plantation in winter, was constructed in 1626. Detailed information about the Heidelberg orangery has come down to us in a book by Salomon de Caus, *Hortus Palatinus (A Garden of the Palatinate)* published in 1620.[7] When de Caus laid out this garden, he arranged for the sixty year old trees from the orangery in the *Herrengarten* to be carried up the hill in their tubs. A temporary winter building, which was taken down every summer, had already been in use in the *Herrengarten*. Now de Caus designed a new building of the same size.

The framework of the building was put up around the trees and boarded with planks before the onset of winter. Wooden shutters could be opened to let in light and air. The building was heated by four stoves so that one could walk about under the trees in all weathers, and since it held more than 400 trees and was over 80 m long, it was quite large enough for a reasonable walk.

The drawback of these buildings was the bad insulation and the need to seal up all joints every time the structures were re-erected. Putting the building up and taking it down was also very expensive, so that an attempt was soon made to reduce the proportion of movable parts by building the north and side walls of stone or brick. This meant that only the roof and the south-facing side had to be covered in the winter.

But it was not only for economic reasons that these temporary wooden structures developed into the permanent orangery towards the end of the seventeenth century. An equally important motive was probably a dissatisfaction with such unpretentious and purely utilitarian buildings. Only a structure of stone or brick could be successfully integrated into the context of a park and castle.

While foreign plants were mainly grown for decorative and culinary purposes at the various courts, private people and botanical gardens were prompted chiefly by their scientific interest to set up plant collections.

The first botanical garden was founded in Padua in 1525, and soon after became the property of the University. After this other botanical gardens came into being all over Europe, many of them connected with the newly founded Universities, like the botanical garden in Pisa in 1544, that in Leipzig, the first in Germany, in 1580, and one in Leyden in 1587.

The botanical gardens exchanged plants, seeds and the information gained from experience, as did the various courts. From the end of the seventeenth century more and more expeditions were sent to all parts of the world to help develop the collections. Not only botanical gardens, but courts and wealthy private people sent plant collectors and botanists into all parts of the world.

In their search for new medicinal drugs, doctors and pharmacists planted special gardens, the *horti medici.*

The first task of the botanists was to define, catalogue and name the growing number of new plants. The results of such research were reported in an ever increasing number of publications. As well as purely botanical works treatises soon appeared dealing with the design and layout of gardens in which the building of orangeries and glasshouses was discussed.

The first illustrations of glasshouses in the literature on the subject date from the end of the seventeenth century. These very early glasshouses, which are said to have existed in botanical gardens at the end of the sixteenth century, were of a fairly modest size, since glass was not only very costly but was only produced in the form of bull's-eye glass and small diamond shaped panes.

Only after Louis Lucas de Nehou had invented the pouring and rolling process in 1688, could sheetglass be manufactured, and by 1700 glass panes 120 cm x 200 cm were being produced. By rationalising the manufacture of glass it became cheaper, so that the extensive glazing of orangeries and greenhouses became practicable.

This brought about the development around 1700 of the classical long and narrow hothouse with the roof and south wall glazed, and the sides and north wall built of masonry.

Duplicate back walls were sometimes built for better heat insulation, at other times a second room was constructed behind and parallel with the greenhouse.

Stoves which could be moved about, and even open fires had been used until the beginning of the eighteenth century, but these now gave way to a new method. One of the drawbacks of using stoves was the unevenness of the warmth, and those plants which stood too close to the source of the heat could be damaged.

A single fire in a heating room behind the north wall of the greenhouse now began to come into use. The smoke was led through heating channels in the wall which radiated a uniform heat. Later, heating channels were laid under the floor.

Straw mats, curtains and wooden shutters were added to regulate the temperature.

There are several illustrations and descriptions of such hothouses in Diderot's *Encyclopédie*. Most of the examples come from Holland. The writer of the article under *serre* (French for glasshouses), says that one should seek information from Dutch and English examples, 'since our nation is not yet enlightened enough about this type of building dedicated to the advance of botany'.[8]

One illustration shows a small Dutch hothouse with a raised and heated back wall. The section of the back wall shows the course of the heating channel. Here heat is conveyed from two sides, while the second

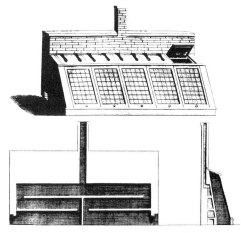

Dutch glasshouse for forcing vines (18th century), from Diderot's *Encyclopédie*.

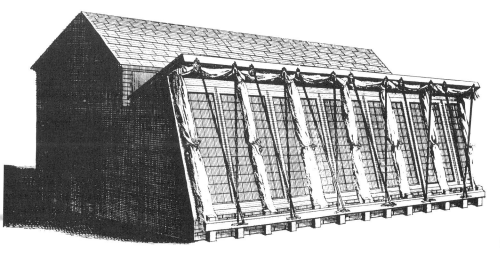

Dutch glasshouse.

11

example has only one fireplace with a small opening which can be seen in the side wall.

The second, larger building is heated by smoke channels under the floor. The glass front can be insulated by curtains attached at the sides, and blinds which can be let down over the curtains. A space between the roof and the ceiling is filled with hay for insulation.

The roof rises towards the front, so that even when the sun is high, the space at the back is well lit. The most important aim in building a greenhouse was to achieve the maximum illumination and greatest possible use of natural warmth.

For this reason much consideration was soon given to finding the most suitable type of roof as well as its most favourable angle. One of the first to research this subject was the botanist and physicist Herman Boerhaave who was director of the Leyden botanical gardens from 1709 to 1730.

Since light rays are partly reflected if they strike a glass pane at an angle, Boerhaave's most important task was to ensure that the light should fall vertically on the glass on the shortest day of the year.

These considerations produced various angles of incidence for different degrees of latitude. Boerhaave succeeded in calculating the angle which was most favourable for Leyden.

Philip Miller, head gardener of the Chelsea Physic Garden in London, based his claim that a glass roof should have two angles on this theory.

It was important that the sun should strike the glass at the front of the building vertically when the sun was low in winter, and the glazed surface of the roof, at an angle of 45°, made the best possible use of the high summer sun. The same consideration led Mackenzie and Loudon to decide, at the beginning of the nineteenth century, that a curved surface was the best type of roof.

The Baroque Orangery

The first period in the history of the orangery ends with the temporary buildings, orange houses which could be taken down and re-erected, which were discussed in the previous chapter. For both economic and aesthetic reasons permanent orangeries began to be built towards the end of the seventeenth century.

De Caus, the builder of the Heidelberg orange house, left plans for a permanent orangery with side and back walls of stone, and only the front wall and the roof to be fitted in the winter. But de Caus's design which was to have replaced the wooden buildings was never carried out.

The same principle was used when the Lower Belvedere in Vienna was built more than a hundred years after the publication of this design. Here, imposing, highly ornamented walls surround the orange plants on three sides. A contemporary illustration shows how the structure was covered over in the autumn. The front was closed by large subdivided windows. The roof was made up of long saddleroofs running parallel with the side walls, each roof equal in width with a window.[9]

But by the time the typical orangery had developed in the first decades of the eighteenth century and spread throughout Europe, it had lost all removable parts. There was nothing temporary in this new type of building which was consciously integrated into the design of castle and park. The facade was designed to fit in with existing buildings, so that what had been an unassuming utility structure became an ornamental building versatile enough to be used for other purposes.

Since the orange trees were not planted directly in the ground but in tubs, it became possible to take them out of doors and put them in front of the orangery in the spring. Alternatively they could be moved about and used as a part of garden design wherever they were wanted.

Other plants, especially myrtles, laurel and pomegranates had in the meantime joined the orange trees in the orangery.

While French orangeries were placed in various parts of the park, German orangeries were always constructed in the same place in relation to the existing buildings.

In the baroque garden, which had developed from the enclosed garden of the middle ages, the orangery formed the furthest boundary between the garden and the open landscape. The relationship between the castle and the orangery dictated its symmetrical groundplan with its structure which was always a taller central building, wings and corner pavilions.

A semi-circular groundplan soon developed from the position of the building at

the end of the garden. The side wings, drawn forward and curved, formed sheltering walls on each side of the orange trees when they were placed in front of the building in the spring. The fact that the central part of the building was set back emphasised the vista from the castle and produced an illusion of greater depth.

The development of this groundplan even led to a breaking up of the building into separate structures, so that where the central part had been there was now, as in French parks, a view of the landscape beyond.

During the baroque period the task of protecting the orange trees through the winter, originally the main object of the orangery, became no more than an excuse for building a companion piece to the castle.

In contrast to the castle, with its outward show of authority, the more informal part of courtly life could be carried on here. By using the adjacent part of the garden, banquets and summer fetes could be held, with the plants in their tubs grouped at will and used as decoration.

In some cases, such as in Kassel, the orangery was not an adjunct of the castle but dominated a park which lay at some distance. Here the orangery took over additional functions since its distance from the castle proper made it necessary to include living quarters and reception rooms.

The building became a kind of 'orangery-castle', and first and foremost a symbol of a courtly way of life, where the question of producing a favourable environment for the plants receded into the background.

While it became technically possible to continue to make the facade more and more transparent, this would have meant renouncing traditional architectural features and going against what had become the main function of the building.

New buildings became necessary when other exotic plants, which needed more light and a higher temperature, became popular and superseded the pre-eminence of the orange.

The culmination of the development of the orangery was reached in the middle of the eighteenth century. Thereafter the decreasing popularity of citrus fruit meant that the glasshouse took over from the orangery; moreover, taste in garden design was also changing. There was no place in the landscape garden for a type of building which was associated in its design, structure and appearance with a formal garden.

Though some orangeries, such as Stüler's building for Charlottenhof Castle (1851–60), were still being erected in the middle of the nineteenth century, they appear more like relics from another age, for courtly, baroque life is never likely to have taken place there.

The evolution of the hothouse proper ran parallel with the development of the courtly orangeries. When it was a question of raising fruit and vegetables, the priority was, of course, to produce a building which let in a maximum of light. To obtain the largest possible glass surface it was necessary to keep the proportion of solid structural components to a minimum. This made wood the most obvious building material.

Beside the lean-to glasshouses which were usually very narrow, other types of planthouses were developed. These may have been derived from the frame structures of the orange houses which could be dismantled. Since glass had in the meantime become available at a reasonable price, it was now possible to consider glazing greenhouses to a much larger extent.

The glasshouse in the illustration is from Volkamer's sequel to the *Nürnbergische Hesperiden*,[10] and is one of the glass buildings in the garden of Herr von Münchhausen

Pineapple house in Schwöbber (early 18th century).

zu Schwöbber in which pineapples were grown for the first time in Germany.

It is here that the origins of the glasshouses of the nineteenth century can be found rather than in the orangeries, for though an attempt was made to adapt transitional forms of the orangery to fulfil new functions, this was only partially successful.

Two disparate aims ran side by side in the construction of glasshouses. One was the development of functional buildings, the other the creation of impressive architecture. Though it soon proved impossible to fulfil both aims, architecture – not only of glasshouses but in general – moved between these two extremes during the whole of the nineteenth century.

Another example worth mentioning, a mixture of architecture and garden design which was built at this time, can still be seen at Potsdam.

Below the castle of Sans Souci (1747) the garden is laid out in terraces. The horizontal surfaces are cultivated, while the vertical parts of the steps are made of glass. The slightly slanting glass surfaces, which run in long rows of steps along the slope, form the front of shallow forcing frames especially suitable for espalier fruit and vines, where even today figs are grown.

Glasshouses of the Nineteenth Century – Origins

Early hothouses and orangeries were at first developed in all the countries of northern Europe, but in the early part of the nineteenth century England began to predominate in this field. 'In no country are materials and labour obtained in greater perfection than in England; in all regular works, coming under the architect or engineer, we generally find little to condemn, and much to admire in the execution of the work.'[11]

This statement from Loudon's *Remarks on the Construction of Hothouses* of 1817 might well be taken for patriotic pride if we did not know that it was justified, and this was recognised without envy on the continent. Many articles in French and German periodicals dealing with the building of hothouses draw the reader's attention to English examples. As far back as Diderot's *Encyclopédie*, England (and Holland) were acknowledged to be the most proficient in this field. France was said not to be 'enlightened'[12] enough, and this was also true of Germany: '. . . they [the German botanical gardens] are generally rich in such plants as will live without any artificial protection, but poor in such as require a stove or a greenhouse.'[13]

The reason for Great Britain's superiority in this field is found not only in its traditional passion for the garden, though England had indeed assumed the lead in garden design in the eighteenth century, initiating the transformation from the geometrical gardens after the French pattern to the landscape garden. English supremacy in hothouse construction lay much more in her advantage, not only in this special field, as the leading economic and industrial country of the nineteenth century. By the time the continent became industrialised – which in Germany, was not until the 1840s – the face of England had already changed fundamentally as a result of industrialisation.

Since even in the eighteenth century England had far-reaching economic freedom, private capital developed very early, and this paved the way for the Industrial Revolution in the last quarter of the eighteenth century. In Germany the guilds did not lose their power until the beginning of the nineteenth century, and the division of the country into small states and principalities also stood in the way of trade and industry.

While Germany still had a feudal structure, England had already developed into a modern industrial society. There was a movement from the countryside to the towns, the population increased enormously and towns grew beyond anything that had been seen before. All these changes necessitated the development of the means of communication. By the middle of the century, England had an extensive railway network and a system of canals for transporting goods and raw materials.

The railway stations and the great spans of the railway bridges are visible proof of the achievement of English engineering of the time. This was mainly due to the progress of iron founding in the last quarter of the eighteenth century.

But there were social changes as well as technical and industrial developments at this time. New social classes, employers and employed, appeared. The power of those representing the old feudal society diminished, though culturally they remained for a long time the models for the rising bourgeoisie.

Aristocratic taste still dominated garden design. The extensive parks which had been cultivated for centuries were still part of the privilege of the aristocracy, and it is here that we find the largest and most costly glasshouses. It was only after the middle of the century that gardens and hothouses came within the means of ordinary people, and then only small ones.

The wish to reduce the structure to glass and its supports, a trend which could already be seen in the simple hothouses of the previous century, now began to be developed. The designers of the new glasshouses dispensed with the architectural elaboration of a stone facade with its windows between massive masonry which kept out much light, and made an effort to reduce the supporting structure of the building as much as possible, thus increasing the transparent surfaces.

Wood was at first the obvious material to take the place of the stone and brick supports. Later iron came into favour. With its help great spans could be bridged, and it proved the most suitable material for the manufacture of building components. Another reason for the emergence of a new type of structure was the improvement in heating techniques. While heating channels in the rear wall were still in common use in the eighteenth century, steam and hotwater heating became accepted at the beginning of the nineteenth century. This did away with the need for a north wall to insulate the greenhouse and reflect heat. With the heating carried through pipes under the floor, it was now possible to glaze the building all the way round. When the north wall became superfluous it was no longer essential for the buildings to face north and south, and many glasshouses were now built to make the largest glazed surfaces face east and west.

These technical developments made a new type of structure possible, and this in turn enabled the buildings to be used for different purposes.

While the first glasshouses, the orangeries, had been built for citrus fruit, and the glasshouses in the gardens of the nobility were used to raise rare fruits for the table, interest now turned to other plants. The orange had fallen from favour and was replaced by tropical plants, first and foremost by palms of which new types were constantly being discovered. This change began around the middle of the eighteenth century when single examples of new tropical plants were at first kept in the traditional buildings. But eventually the tropical plants, which not only had to be overwintered like the oranges, but needed more light and heat, made special buildings necessary.

A predominantly economic interest in exotic vegetation also provided a stimulus for intensive botanical research.

The British Empire was, in the nineteenth century, the largest colonial empire. The British colonies in Asia, Africa, America and Australia covered a quarter of the surface of the earth.

The colonies, the most important market for Britain's manufactured articles, supplied raw materials and much newly discovered agricultural produce. This created a great deal of interest in the exploration of the vegetation of the colonial countries. Many plants which were first and foremost useful to the economy can still be seen in the palm house at Kew. They yielded crops like coffee, cocoa, bananas, rubber and, above all, cotton for the English textile industry. Palms were of great importance in tropical countries, producing not only food but also materials used for clothing and shelter.

Thus the age of colonialism was also the heyday of botany. Starting in 1772, the Royal Botanic Gardens at Kew sent plant collectors and expeditions into the whole world. William Aiton's three-volume catalogue published in 1789, the *Hortus Kewensis*, already listed 5500 exotic plants which were growing in the gardens.

Not only botanical gardens, but wealthy private people and the courts, were patrons of science. The Prussian government, the Austrian Emperor and the King of Bavaria financed botanical expeditions.

'The late King of Bavaria, at whose private charges Drs. Spix and Martius were for a long time occupied in exploring the riches of Brazil, did not cease to extend this patronage to them after their return, but nobly provided the means of making the world acquainted with the results of their discoveries, in a manner equally worth of the monarch and the man of science. The work on Brazilian palms, by Dr. Martius, is one of the most splendid and perfect botanical productions the world ever beheld.'[14]

King Leopold II of the Belgians, for example, used the exploration of foreign parts of the world as a search for new territories which could be profitably colonised. The society for the 'Exploration and Civilisation of Africa' which he founded in 1876 and which sent Stanley to explore the Congo, was chiefly concerned with ruthless economic exploitation. Science was no more than a pretext.

These botanical explorations were supported not only by the public and private gardens, which at the beginning of the nineteenth century appeared everywhere, but also by the horticultural societies like the London Horticultural Society and the Prussian Horticultural Society. These associations corresponded with each other and exchanged plants.

They usually owned their own gardens, and the membership subscriptions and entrance fees contributed to the cost of expensive glasshouses.

The Horticultural Society which was founded in Kensington in 1802 acquired a garden in Chiswick in 1822 in which glasshouses and 'a magnificent conservatory' were erected.[15]

The Royal Botanic Society had a garden in Regent's Park in London, and before the Large Palm House at Kew was finished opened its own palm house there, designed by the same architect.

There were also floral societies in even the smallest towns, dedicated to raising flowers, and they exhibited what they grew in annual flowershows.

The outstanding plant among the exotic vegetation raised in European hothouses at this time was certainly the palm. As early as the 1830s buyers could choose from between 150 to 170 different kinds of palms at the Hackney Botanic Nursery in London which had been founded by Conrad Loddiges in 1771. When Loddiges' nursery closed in 1854, Paxton bought the whole stock for the Crystal Palace which had then already been moved to Sydenham.

The director of the botanical garden in Nymphenburg, Dr. Martius, who has already been mentioned, estimated the number of different types of palms as around a thousand. He described the trees in quite unscientific but characteristic enthusiasm of his time: 'Palms, the noble offspring of Terra and Phoebus, are natives of those happy countries within the tropics, where the rays of the latter are ever beaming.'[16]

The palm became a symbol of the longing for those 'happy countries'. This love of everything exotic answered a need which had already shown itself in the gardens of the eighteenth century. The garden had become a land of illusion, a place of refuge from the civilized world.

An illusion of unfamiliar parts of the world and of the past was created with the help of exotic and historical settings. Chinese pavilions, Egyptian pyramids, Gothic chapels, the ruins of Roman aqueducts and the bogus graves of poets and philosophers of the classical period excited the imagination and awoke a longing for the Golden Age and the lost innocence of the Garden of Eden.

The geometrical gardens which proclaimed the human spirit's domination of nature began to be replaced by the landscape garden which tried artificially to recreate a lost purity.

In the Dukes of Devonshire's garden at Chatsworth, the geometrical flowerbeds gave way to great lawns, terraces were turned back into grassy slopes, straight paths were transformed into twisting walks. The symmetrical patterns of the flowerbeds had to give way to 'natural' grouping. The transformation of the garden at Chatsworth began under the direction of Lancelot 'Capability' Brown, and was continued in the nineteenth century by Joseph Paxton. Both these men wanted to create a garden that was literally 'picturesque', where the ideal landscapes of Poussin and Claude Lorrain often served as models. Artificial waterfalls, cascades and grottos were as important in creating this picturesque effect as the architectural parts of the setting.

In some French gardens, where the English example was very quickly adopted, even the glasshouses were built in exotic and historical styles. Illustrations of an orangery and a hothouse in the Chinese style in Le Désert, of around 1770, are still in existence.

The picturesque and exotic styles were considered frivolous exceptions to the classicist rule and are confined to garden buildings. Exotic styles for other buildings only became popular later in the course of an eclecticism which embraced architecture as a whole.

Transition from Orangery to Buildings of Iron and Glass

'The culture of palms, as Mr. Loudon justly observes, is less a matter of nicety than expense. They require a powerful moist heat, a large mass of rich earth in the pot, tub or bed, and ample space for the leaves. As they are of remarkably slow growth, a stove devoted to their culture does not require to exceed the common height at first; but, to admit the tree palms to display their character, it would require to have the roof elevated by degrees to sixty, eighty, or a hundred feet. It is much to be wished that some spirited man of wealth would, in these times of peace and leisure, distinguish himself by palm culture, of which Messrs. Loddiges have, much to their honour, set the first example.'

Charles MacIntosh, 1838[17]

Some of the first large planthouses, such as those at Alton Towers, Staffordshire, at Syon Park, London, and in Kassel-Wilhelmshöhe still exist to this day. These buildings were constructed to meet the demands of exotic tropical plants and at the same time to preserve the appearance of the architectural orangery and keep alive its courtly connotation into the new century. These hothouses were built on the principle of the orangery, but with a glazed roof, a facade where less masonry and more glass was used, and a dome above the central part.

The buildings retain the characteristic groundplan of the orangery and attempt to preserve its original architectural features such as a facade divided by columns, though the use of the building had changed. In Kassel (pages 52–4) the whole facade is divided into rectangular window panes, though the diameter of the semi-circular columns is reduced to a minimum. At Syon (pages 48–51), on the other hand, masonry and windows are in about equal proportions except in the curved wings which join the central building to the pavilions.

Without this large proportion of masonry it would not have been possible for the building's architect, Charles Fowler, to design it in the Italian style.

The complex of glasshouses built in 1825 for the Earl of Shrewsbury at Alton Towers had seven glass domes, and there was an open gallery between the central building and the side pavilions.

Loudon described this building as follows: 'The style may be considered as Grecian or Roman. The back wall is of opaque masonry, and the front has stone piers and architraves, filled in with cast and wrought iron and copper sashes. The roof and dome are also of ironwork, and copper, glazed. The whole is richly ornamented with vases and sculptures, and the domes are profusely gilt.'[18]

Loudon mentions another gothic glasshouse which he saw there during his visit in 1831 and which he said 'had the appearance of a plain cathedral'. The heating in these buildings, on the other hand, was quite modern with heating pipes running under the paths.

But gardeners did not, on the whole, like these 'architectural hothouses' (a concept formulated by Loudon), since they did not produce the best environment for the growth of plants.

In his book of 1838, *The Greenhouse, Hothouse and Stove*, MacIntosh, though he admired the Duke of Northumberland's splendid complex at Syon, which was completely in keeping with the surrounding buildings, said that, 'so far as plant culture alone is concerned, no arrangement can be more unsuccessful.'[19]

The Ward, Lock & Co. travel guide of 1851 also complains that while some of the plants in the building are 'exceedingly rare, they apparently are labouring under the effects produced by an overcrowded apartment'.

But the potential of the new technique can already be seen in the iron and glass dome of the glasshouse, almost 20 m high, built at Syon between 1820 and 1827. Loudon's experimental buildings erected after 1818 used these technical advances, creating buildings which, above all, fulfilled the functions of a greenhouse without added ornamentation. Loddiges too had a palmhouse designed by Loudon in his commercial nursery and here it would, of course, have been inappropriate to sacrifice the well-being of the plants to a grandiose appearance. The attempt to combine the two was bound to lead to a dead-end.

Later examples of the kind of structure derived from the orangery are the buildings in the moorish style erected in 1842–6 in the Wilhelma in Stuttgart (pages 64–7). Here only the central building uses masonry, the wings and corner pavilions are of iron and glass.

Conservatory at Alton Towers (1825), Robert Abraham.

New Construction Potentialities

The 'new' materials, iron and glass, were of crucial importance in the technological development of building in the nineteenth century. Though both materials had been used since classical times, they were 'new' in the sense that it was not until the eighteenth century that it became possible to manufacture them industrially in large quantities. Now that coke rather than charcoal, which was only available in limited quantities, could be used in the smelting of iron ore, the way was open for the development of the iron industry. Cast-iron chimneys for the new steam engines had been produced as far back as 1718. The quality of raw and cast-iron was further improved by the process known as 'puddling' which Henry Cort patented in 1783. By stirring in air, carbon was extracted from the iron, and wrought iron was obtained, and this was far superior to the brittle cast-iron.

Iron was at first only employed to manufacture machinery, but by the last quarter of the eighteenth century it began to be used in buildings. The iron bridge over the Severn, jointly constructed in 1777–9 by the iron-founder Abraham Darby and the architect Thomas Farnolls Pritchard, can still be seen in the town in central England now known as Ironbridge.

After this, innumerable iron bridges were built in the course of the extension of the road and railway network. Iron was also used in the construction of factories from the 1790s, though, hidden in the masonry, it is much less easily seen than in bridge construction. Boulton & Watt, best known as manufacturers of steam engines, built a textile factory in Salford in 1799 which was one of the first iron-frame constructions, and this type of building soon became popular. Rickman & Cragg even used an iron frame to build three churches in Liverpool between 1813 and 1816.

Building in iron, which continued to be chiefly developed in England and France, was mostly confined to bridges and railway stations, exhibition halls, glasshouses and business premises such as arcades and warehouses. Only much later, after the middle of the nineteenth century, was iron increasingly used in traditional types of buildings. A modern iron structure is, for example, hidden in Garnier's baroque Paris Opera House (1861–74). The improvement in the materials was one of the crucial elements in the continued development in building techniques. In the early bridges as well as in Loudon's glasshouses, cast-iron was only used in conjunction with wrought iron. Because of its high carbon content, the cast-iron was very brittle and could only be used under pressure, so that wherever parts of the structure had to stand stress and curvature, wrought iron was used. On the other hand, forged parts could not be manufactured as efficiently as cast parts. Henry Bessemer's subsequent invention of steel did away with such composite structures.

Large panes of glass were first manufactured by a process of pouring and rolling around 1700 as already mentioned. But in the early nineteenth century much of the glass on the market was evidently still produced by the old process. Panes manufactured in this way were small and had an uneven, often bubbled, surface which was blamed by many gardeners for the fact that when plants stood close to the panes of glass they were singed by the sun, the bubbles acting as a burning-glass.

The early glasshouses in Bicton Gardens (pages 55–7) and Wollaton Hall (pages 58–9) were glazed with these small panes. If this process had been used on a larger scale, the many iron ribs would have made building with glass much too expensive.

Cast glass was also still imperfect at this time, since it was matt on one side.

The quality of glass only improved after the pouring and rolling process had been perfected. When (in 1845 in England) the glass tax was abolished, the manufacture of large panes became profitable, and glass ceased to be a luxury.

While only small panes were at first used, and those mostly in greenhouses, glass soon became an efficient material for roofing large expanses in other new types of building such as railway stations, arcades and exhibition halls.

John Claudius Loudon's Spherical Glasshouses

'When subsequent improvements in communicating heat, and in ventilation, shall have rendered the artificial climates produced equal or superior to those which they imitate, then will such an appendage to a family seat be not less useful in a medical point of view, than elegant and luxurious as a lounge for exercise or entertainment in inclement weather. Perhaps the time may arrive when such artificial climates will not only be stocked with appropriate birds, fishes, and harmless animals, but with examples of the human species from the different countries imitated, habited in their particular costumes, and who may serve as gardeners or curators of the different productions. But this subject is too new and strange to admit of discussion, without incurring the ridicule of general readers.'

John Claudius Loudon, 1817[20]

John Claudius Loudon (1783–1843) exerted, through his innumerable articles, books and publications, a great influence on the taste of his time as far as architecture, interior decoration and garden design were concerned. He also contributed considerably to the art of building with iron and glass. Born in Scotland, Loudon became apprenticed to a landscape gardener when he was fifteen. With exceptional ambition and application he laid the foundations of a knowledge of botany, chemistry, agriculture and architecture, as well as learning several languages which stood him in good stead in his later travels.

He went to London in 1803 and began to work as garden designer on his own account. At the same time his first writings were published.

Many of his projects and suggestions on questions of town planning show his interest in social matters, as for example his proposal for a Green Belt for the ever-growing city of London. He was also the author of progressive proposals for abolishing social injustices in the English school system. But he became known chiefly for his publications such as the *Encyclopaedia of Gardening* of 1822, an extensive work which expressed opinions on all theoretical and practical aspects of horticulture and garden design, and which contained not only a history of the garden but also descriptions of the foremost European gardens. Many of the drawings and accounts were the result of several European journeys which took him, sometimes under adventurous circumstances, as far as Russia.

Most of his publications after his marriage in 1830 were written in collaboration with his wife Jane who had herself already had some literary success. His next large publication was the *Encyclopaedia of Cottage, Farm and Villa Architecture and Furniture* (1833) which became the most important work of reference for architects, building contractors and furniture makers, and which greatly influenced Victorian taste until the end of the century.

There are also suggestions for furnishing restaurants in this book, as well as recommendations for building glasshouses, and illustrations of country houses in gothic, Italian and 'castle' styles.

Thus Loudon contributed considerably to the great variety of styles of the time. He edited the *Gardener's Magazine*, was editor from 1834 of *The Architectural Magazine* as well as of a long list of other publications. Loudon, who also continued to design glasshouses and gardens, worked ceaselessly without consideration for his health. He died at sixty as the result of pneumonia, but surely also from overwork.

Under the heading, 'Of the Principles of Design in Plant-houses' (*Encyclopaedia of Gardening*), Loudon traced step by step those principles of construction which sprang from the need to produce an artificial climate suitable for the respective plants.[21] Since the chief aim when building a hothouse was to let in a maximum of light, he asked that there should be as little masonry as possible. He stressed the importance of the light striking the glass panes as vertically as possible, since this avoids reflections. When light strikes the glass diagonally, much of it is reflected back and lost. These considerations led to a building style which was first discussed in a lecture to the members of the Horticultural Society by Sir George Mackenzie in 1815.

The title of the lecture was 'On the Form which the Glass of a Forcinghouse ought to have in order to receive the greatest possible quantity of the Rays from the Sun'.[22] The result of Mackenzie's research was that the most suitable shape of the glass roof was 'a hemispherical figure'.[23] The section of the spherical roof should run parallel with the course of the sun, so that most of the rays would strike vertically both in the summer and when the sun is low in the winter. If the groundplan of the building was semicircular, the result, a quarter sphere, would face south and receive morning, noon and evening sun.

Mackenzie's lecture triggered off Loudon's preoccupation with spherical glass buildings of this kind. In 1818 he erected a series of prototypes of buildings according to curvilinear principles on his land in Bayswater, and these were the first of their kind in England. He published the first results of this work in 1817, in his 'Remarks on the Construction of Hothouses'. He considered semi- and quarter spheres the most suitable shapes, also buildings with a semi-elliptical groundplan and semi-elliptical section.

Pointed glass dome, John Claudius Loudon.

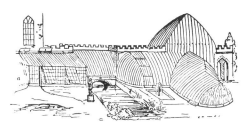

Rectangular glasshouse with curved roof and rounded ends, John Claudius Loudon.

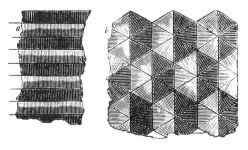

Experimental buildings in Bayswater (1815–18), John Claudius Loudon.

'Ridge and furrow' and pyramid roof, John Claudius Loudon.

Half-dome, W. & D. Bailey.

Serre courbe par M. Bailey

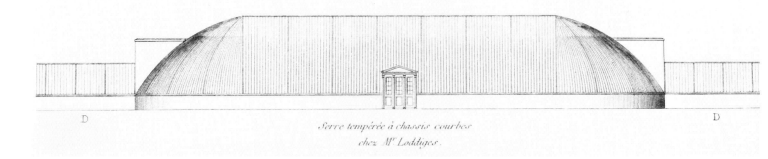

To guarantee that the water ran off satisfactorily, Loudon had his domes and half-domes come to a point at the top. Rectangular groundplans with rounded ends and curved roofs were derived from these shapes.

Though Loudon considered the dome the best possible shape, he had to admit that a building with a curved skin was more expensive than one with straight surfaces. He therefore suggested a polygonal shape as an alternative, the circle becoming a polygon. A hothouse with a polygonal groundplan was illustrated as far back as 1714 in Christopher Volkamer's *Nürnberger Hesperiden*. This building stood in Volkamer's own garden in Nürnberg-Gostenhof. [24]

The glass skin of the building illustrated above was smooth, but Loudon suggested two other roof constructions, the 'ridge and furrow' roof, and a roof made of hexagonal or octagonal pyramids.

While he recommended the latter principle only for smooth roof surfaces, he showed a spherical roof which was constructed on the 'ridge and furrow' principle. The shape of this building was the same as that shown on page 19 (2nd ill. from top). The rectangular part of the groundplan was covered by a curved 'ridge and furrow' roof but the ends, two quarter-circles on the groundplan, were covered in smooth glass panes. This pleated roof had two advantages. Firstly it could bear a greater weight of snow in winter than a roof with a smooth skin, and secondly the sun would fall vertically most of the morning

and afternoon on one of the surfaces which would be exposed to it at an angle of 90°.

Paxton later took over the 'ridge and furrow' roof for his buildings, chiefly because of its stability. Loudon himself did not develop this building method any further.

The glasshouses designed by him for his clients after 1818 all had smooth roofs. The first building to use a 'ridge and furrow' roof as well as a curved surface was Paxton's Great Conservatory at Chatsworth (1836). Loudon had, in 1816, developed a spherical curved wrought iron bar for his buildings, but transferred the rights to the commercial exploitation of this invention to the firm of W. & D. Bailey in London in 1818, and they built many glasshouses from his designs in subsequent years. Two examples are the glasshouse of the Loddiges nursery, and a semi-circular dome which was built in 1824 to stand against a north wall.

At Bretton Hall, Yorkshire, a glass dome of imposing size was built for Mrs. Beaumont in 1827, but this was unfortunately sold and demolished after the owner's death. This building, the total cost of which was £14,000, was approximately 18 m in height and had a diameter of 30 m, and it was built entirely of iron and glass. Even the base which held the lower ventilation shutters was made of metal. As so often, this was a structure of both cast and wrought iron. All vertical supports were of cast-iron, while the ribs were of wrought iron.

As well as the ventilating shutters in the base, windows below the springing of the

Greenhouse in the nursery of Conrad Loddiges in Hackney, W. & D. Bailey.

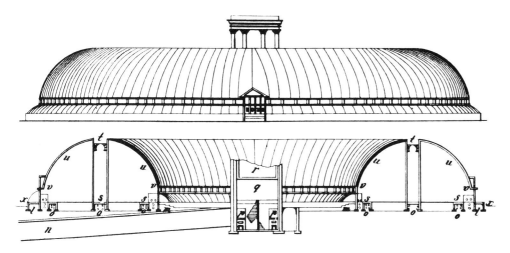

Project for the Botanical Garden in Birmingham (1831), John Claudius Loudon.

upper dome and a fanlight hidden under the top coronet could be opened to air the building. A heating house at some distance produced the steam for the pipes under the floor.

Loudon stressed that the thin sash-bars of about 1.25 x 5 cm (½ x 2 in) needed no additional support.

The upper dome, on the other hand, was carried on iron supports.

Yet when the panes of glass had been fitted, the structure was found to possess the necessary rigidity: 'When the ironwork was put up, before it was glazed, the slightest wind put the whole of it in motion from the base to the summit; and so much alarm did this create in the party for whom it was to be put up. . . that the contractors for the work, Messrs. W. & D. Bailey, of Holborn, London, were obliged to covenant to keep it in repair for a certain number of years. As soon as the glass was put in, however, it was found to become perfectly firm and strong. . .'[25]

There is reason to believe that the palm house at Bicton Gardens (pages 55–7) which still stands today was built by the firm of W. & D. Bailey from a design by Loudon.

In 1831 Loudon submitted designs for the Botanical Gardens in Birmingham which had been founded under the chairmanship of Matthew Boulton. He produced two alternative projects for a glasshouse.

The first design envisaged a glass ring with a tower in the centre. The tower was to contain a heating installation and the water tank for a sprinkling mechanism. There was to be an underground tunnel through which fuel could be conveyed. In the roof ridge of the glasshouse ring, Loudon arranged for a walkway from which straw mats could be unrolled to add to the insulation. For the second design Loudon suggested a more elaborate conical structure 60 m in diameter and 30 m in height, which would be partitioned into four sections with different climatic conditions. In the centre of the building a glass cylinder, which went up to the roof, was to house the tallest tropical trees. A spiral ramp was to wind around the glass cylinder, giving access to galleries at various levels. Unfortunately neither of the two designs was carried out.

Such designs, which show Loudon to have been far in advance of his time, demonstrate the realisation of one of his aims which was that 'every building should appear to be what it is, and every part of an edifice ought to indicate externally its particular use'. Elsewhere he placed 'the beauties . . . of use and truth' above the mere display of various styles. Architecture 'as an art of taste' would of course add another dimension of beauty to a building which satisfies functional demands.

He did not reject the use of historical or exotic styles, but wanted to place these 'abstract principles of composition' which are common to every kind of architecture above a grasp of prevailing styles.[26]

Loudon did not consider his 'functionalist' ideas incompatible with current architectural practice but liked to think that his aim of architectural honesty could go hand in hand with the stylistic pluralism he too advocated.

Conservatory at Bretton Hall (1827),
W. & D. Bailey.

Joseph Paxton's Glasshouses at Chatsworth

While we see Loudon as the pioneer in glasshouse construction at a time when building with iron and glass was at the experimental stage, we connect Joseph Paxton's name with the era of the development of iron and glass structures. Many of Loudon's ideas were never carried out. His largest projects, the two designs for the Botanical Gardens in Birmingham, were never executed.

Though Loudon was the first to publish the design for the 'ridge and furrow' roof in his *Encyclopaedia*, he never used his invention in any of his glasshouses. It was left for Joseph Paxton to try out this type of construction in the glasshouses he built for the Duke of Devonshire at Chatsworth after 1828.

Paxton was born in 1803, the seventh son of a farmer, and from his fifteenth year worked in various gardens where he taught himself everything connected with his profession. From 1822 he worked in the gardens of the Horticultural Society in Chiswick, where the Duke of Devonshire met him and, in 1826, offered him the post of head gardener at Chatsworth. Though his sphere of work grew through the years, Paxton remained in the Duke's service until his employer's death in 1858.

At Chatsworth his duties soon went beyond those of a gardener. He was not only engaged in the reorganisation of the gardens, but also represented the business interests of the Duke with whom he was on friendly terms. Paxton thus had the chance of continuing to improve his education, especially during the many journeys he undertook, some in the company of his employer. He soon became financially independent, partly through commissions he carried out as landscape designer and architect, but also through speculative ventures in connection with the development of the railway network and the new housing estates where he was also involved in the planning.

Schemes like Prince's Park in Liverpool and Birkenhead Park represented new types of building speculation which, by connecting public parks with villa suburbs, made the value of building sites rise steeply after the completion of the park, so that they could be sold at great profit.

Besides all this, he also edited *Paxton's Magazine of Botany* from 1834, and *The Gardener's Chronicle* from 1841.

The acceptance in 1850 of his design for the exhibition hall of the International Exhibition led to the culmination of his extraordinary career. Though an outsider, he succeeded with his design for the Crystal Palace in breaking into a field which had been dominated by engineers and architects.

But the new concept behind the Crystal Palace did not come about by chance. It followed naturally from the construction and manufacturing methods developed at Chatsworth. It was there that Paxton had tried out the first 'ridge and furrow' roof in 1832. He had, as a matter of fact, used mostly wood for the framework of his glasshouses from the very start. Other buildings using the same principle followed, among them a structure with an elliptical roof, and the palm house for Loddiges for whom Loudon had worked before Paxton.

Conservatory at Chatsworth (1836–41), John Paxton. Groundplan and section.

In 1836 the new conservatory at Chatsworth was begun, and this was to surpass all other structures of its kind in England in both area and span, even taking into account the large glazed roofs of the railway stations.

At Chatsworth a glass roof of a least 20 m (67 ft) in height rose above a rectangular area of 84.5 m x 37.5 m (123 ft x 277 ft). The cross-section of the roof was like that of a basilica, with its barrel-vault standing on cast-iron columns.

The local *Derbyshire Courier* printed the following description at the time:

'This immense structure is composed of glass panes manufactured especially for it, placed in iron framework, of the lightest apparent kind, but as subsequent trials have proved, of the most firm and substantial description. The length of the erection is nearly 300 feet, its height above 70, and its width 150. It covers nearly an acre of ground, through the centre of which is the carriage road, and the tubes for the hot water which regulate the required temperature measure six miles. A light, but beautiful gallery, erected at the base of the dome, and which traverses the entire building, enables the spectator to review the whole of the interior from various points. The access to the gallery is by steps, placed with admirable taste in the midst of rock work, in the fissures of which are plants, apparently natural productions. A tunnel surrounds the whole edifice, by which access is obtained to the stoves and pipes, and rails are laid down to convey the coals per train, and supply the necessary heat. The interior contains a vast number of trees and plants, many of them of gigantic proportions, and the rarest of tropical growth. Birds of varied and exquisite beauty, whose delicate structure could not endure the rigours of our climate, are seen flying about; and pools of water, in which plants suited to the required purpose have been encouraged to grow, contain gold, silver, and other fish. In this structure may be seen the largest crystal yet found in the world. . .'[27]

The enormous building was to have been considerably enlarged by the addition of two wings. This would have given it more or less the same shape as the palm house by Decimus Burton and Richard Turner at Kew (pages 68–73).

Some of the plans of Paxton's conservatory are marked with Decimus Burton's initials, but it is not clear what his contribution to the design was.

When the building was finished in 1841, the total cost had added up to more than £ 33,000. But it did not have an iron frame as the *Derbyshire Courier* mistakenly maintained. This immense structure was made of wood, and only the pillars and the gallery were of cast-iron. The cast-iron columns were hollow and led the rainwater away from the wooden roof-arches and window sashes which acted as gutters. Since Paxton needed a great number of these special wooden sections, he constructed a steam-driven sash-cutting machine especially to rationalise the manufacture of these parts. This process was also used during the construction of the Crystal Palace, for its 'ridge and furrow' roof was also made of wooden sections. The pleated roof of the conservatory was also supported by additional curved beams of laminated wood. The columns in the transept of the Crystal Palace were also made of wood.

The size of the conservatory at Chatsworth caused a considerable stir at the time. Its

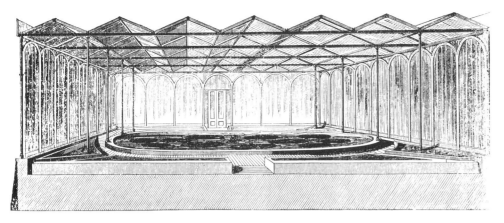

Waterplant house at Chatsworth (1850), Joseph Paxton.

scale comes vividly to life when one reads that during the Queen's visit in 1848 the whole company drove through the artificially lit building in open carriages. The impression Paxton's building made on the royal visitors stimulated a desire for a similar glasshouse for the Botanic Gardens at Kew.

The conservatory at Chatsworth was demolished after the First World War, since its upkeep had become too expensive for the descendants of the sixth Duke of Devonshire.

The glasshouse for water plants built at Chatsworth in 1850 does not exist any more either. Paxton had acquired a Victoria Regia plant in 1849 and found a place for it in one of the existing glasshouses. But the water-lily grew so fast that it soon became necessary to build a special house for it. Another glasshouse was therefore built, this time with a flat, 'ridge and furrow' roof, and Paxton patented this method the same year.

This building showed even more clearly than earlier structures that Paxton's method of using a small number of prefabricated parts could be used for buildings of any dimension. The various identical building components could be reproduced in quantity, and once this method was adopted, the basic concept of the structure of the Crystal Palace was already fully developed.

Paxton was the first to succeed in bringing the Victoria Regia into flower in England. With publicity always in mind, he gave the first bloom to the Queen after whom the plant was named.

Specialised Buildings

Once the Victoria Regia had successfully bloomed, the plant became the sensation of botanical gardens all over Europe. In 1862 a waterplant house designed by Turner was built at Kew. There was already such a building in the botanical gardens in Brussels which had been erected in 1854. This is still in existence, though it has been moved elsewhere (pages 60–1). Other, smaller Victoria Regia houses were built at Leyden, Munich and Berlin. All these buildings have square, octagonal or round groundplans and were built over a central water basin. The glass roof was set fairly low over the basin, so that the interior could be well heated. The plants, which come from the tropical region of the Amazon, need a great deal of warmth, and the water too had to be heated.

Loudon suggested how one might simulate the flow of water in such a basin. In his design for an ideal hothouse for waterplants, a round building with a pointed dome, machinery under the central basin made the plants growing on a rotating table revolve in the water.[28]

Apart from the Victoria Regia house there were other hothouses at Chatsworth which each fulfilled some special climatic demand. This great estate had probably the largest collection of glasshouses in the whole of England around 1860. There were three orchid houses as well as houses for plants from 'New Holland' (Australia), conifer houses, and hothouses for vines, cherries, strawberries, peaches, melons, cucumbers and mushrooms.

Even at the time of the baroque courts, there had been buildings for special plants in addition to the orangeries. In the eighteenth century special houses for pineapples were much in favour. One of the people who is known to have enjoyed raising this fruit was Frederick the Great (page 14).

The camellia which came from eastern Asia became fashionable in the nineteenth century, and hothouses for raising camellias were built. There is still a remarkable example of a camellia house in the park of Wollaton Hall near Nottingham (pages 58–9).

Waterplant house (1822), John Claudius Loudon.

Prefabricated Building Parts and Modular Co-ordination

Paxton's Crystal Palace is generally thought of as the first systematically prefabricated building, though these concepts had already been tried out in his earlier glasshouses. The Great Exhibition Building in fact represents the climax of fifty years of the development of prefabrication, for when the International Exhibition took place in 1851, there were well-established firms amongst the exhibitors, like E. T. Bellhouse of Manchester, who had long specialised in the manufacture of prefabricated iron buildings.

It is not surprising that the history of prefabrication began in Britain, for Great Britain led the world in industrial development.[29]

The British Colonies provided the initial impetus towards the manufacture of prefabricated buildings. Since there were not enough qualified workmen nor an efficient building industry in the colonies, some manufacturers conceived the idea of offering emigrants inexpensive living quarters which could be shipped in pieces and, even after being put up, could be dismantled again and re-erected in another place. From 1790 on, prefabricated wooden frame buildings were sent to Australia, and around 1830 'Manning's Portable Colonial Cottage' was a well-known proprietary name. Most of these buildings were made of wood and canvas.

When, around 1820, cast-iron and corrugated iron began to be manufactured, they soon replaced these less durable materials. As early as 1807 a cast-iron bridge, manufactured by the famous Coalbrookdale, Company, had been shipped to Jamaica. From the time of the dispatch of the first 'Colonial Cottage', the range of prefabricated buildings on offer from British manufacturers had grown steadily. Besides the large corrugated iron sheds for the London docks, whole warehouses, factories, and even lighthouses and churches were prefabricated. Most of these buildings went overseas since there was no great demand for them in England, and the corrugated iron buildings, with their unattractive exteriors, would have been difficult to sell at home.

Sometimes the demand for prefabricated buildings arose overnight. When the goldrush in California started in 1849, there was a sudden demand for every kind of building. Bellhouse, the Manchester manufacturers, shipped complete warehouses to San Francisco.

The palm house in San Francisco's Golden Gate Park (pages 98–9) was also imported from England.

In the 1840s and 50s new firms specialising in prefabrication appeared constantly. In 1853 Samuel Hemming dispatched six prefabricated churches to Australia, and two years later one of their churches, faced in corrugated iron, was even put up in Kensington. Such large buildings were usually tested by being erected in the factory grounds before being taken apart again and finally packed in cases. Robertson & Lister of Glasgow held a great ball in an iron warehouse which was then taken to pieces and shipped to Melbourne. While these structures were widely advertised, such an event served to make them even better known to a public eager for such novelties.

When the firm of Bellhouse exhibited a customs house destined for Peru in the grounds of its foundry, 25 000 people came to see it in the ten days it was on show. But foreign competition soon appeared in the South American market. The company headed by the French engineer Gustave Eiffel began to put up harbour and customs buildings as well as iron churches.

When Bellhouse presented a prospectus of his output at the Crystal Palace in 1851, prefabricated iron buildings had become so socially acceptable that Prince Albert ordered an iron ball-room for Balmoral Castle. He was not the first royal customer for such a building: the firm of Laycock of Liverpool had supplied King Eyambo of Nigeria with an iron palace in 1843.

At the time of the Great Exhibition of 1851, the Crystal Palace itself was the visible proof of the advanced state of English technology. How successful the building was is shown by the fact that other crystal palaces were soon built in Munich and New York.

The jury had found no satisfactory entry amongst the 245 designs submitted to the competition for the building to house the 'Great Exhibition of the Works of Industry of all Nations'. This gave Paxton the chance to submit a design he had completed in eight days. When he finally received the commission for the building, it was not so much because he knew the right people as because his design got the building committee out of a difficulty, for when Paxton was given the commission in July 1850, there were only nine months before the opening date of the exhibition.

A building of this size could never have been finished in time if it had been constructed by traditional methods. It was 30 m high, more than 560 m long, and about 1250 m wide, and it covered an exhibition site of at least a 100 000 m^2 (18 acres).

Only by the teamwork of the many specialists, chiefly engineers of the firm of Fox and Henderson, and by restricting the design to a limited number of standardised mass-produced building parts of wood and cast-iron was it possible to keep to the proposed time schedule.

Since the building was assembled from prefabricated parts, there was no difficulty in taking it down again, and the parts could be re-used for a structure of the same or another shape in some other place.

Crystal Palace, London (1851), Joseph Paxton.

Soon after the exhibition, Paxton suggested transforming the Crystal Palace into a 'Wintergarden and Garden under Glass' with enough space for people not only to go for walks, but also for riding and driving in carriages.

When Parliament voted against buying the Crystal Palace as a public wintergarden, Paxton had already formed a joint stock company which bought the building and had it re-erected by Fox and Henderson. It was improved and enlarged at great cost, and opened at Sydenham in 1854. It was destroyed by fire in 1936. The Crystal Palace was a novelty not only because of its radical use of industrial prefabrication for an architectural project, but also because of the feeling of space which the building produced.

There had never been an interior of such dimensions. By the recurring use of the same building components, an impression of infinity was created, while the fact that the walls were transparent gave the illusion that the outside world was part of the building. There was even enough headroom for the tall elms which had been part of the building site to be left standing.

While at first manufacturers had mostly developed complete buildings, the British iron founders then set about producing standard building parts which could be put together in any number of combinations and made a complete 'building set'.

The iron foundries were mostly centred in Scotland which still dominated the market at the time. One of the best known was Walter MacFarlane & Co., a foundry which had been started in Glasgow in 1850. Their two-volume catalogue of 1882 contains more than 700 pages of cast-iron parts for the building trade. Everything imaginable from rain gutters, railings, doors, stairs, street lamps, school benches, baths, street urinals, pillars, plinths and brackets, to complete porches, verandas, bandstands and, of course, glasshouses and wintergardens was offered for sale.

All these parts could be obtained in standardised sizes. Basic building parts like pillars, brackets and plinths could be ordered in a variety of decorative patterns. MacFarlane's alone offered around 140 cast-iron pillars, differing in style and measurement.

The buildings illustrated in the catalogue, which were assembled from the 'building-sets', were only examples to show the almost unlimited combinations that this system could produce.

Under the heading 'Conservatories', there are several examples of buildings, starting with small conservatories suitable as an addition to a house, and going on to huge glasshouses with central domes and side wings which could be adapted to any size and any type of groundplan.

MacFarlane's were 'possibly the first mail-order house in the prefabrication business'.[30]

Some manufacturers specialised in glasshouses. Jones and Clark were one of the first companies which erected greenhouses from prefabricated cast-iron parts. The camellia house at Wollaton Hall (pages 58–9), which was built in 1823 and still stands, is an impressive example.

While prefabricated greenhouses were still the exception in the first half of the nineteenth century, mass production of such buildings had become the rule in the seven-

Wood and glass greenhouse made by the firm of Cranston around 1863.

ties and eighties. Owning a greenhouse or conservatory was originally a luxury only the well-to-do could afford, but when greenhouses became available by 'mail-order', this luxury came within the means of ordinary people.

In 1858 Paxton, who had in the meantime become 'Sir Joseph', patented a simple tent-shaped greenhouse of wood and glass which could be folded up. This was meant to appeal to the general public, and the company which sold the greenhouse advertised it with the slogan 'Hothouses for the Millions'.

As industrialisation continued, a middle class which constituted the most important customer for industrial products had developed in the towns, and it was at this middle class that the advertisements were aimed.

Paxton's design was originally derived from a commission he had carried out for the British Government. During the Crimean War of 1854–5 a large number of cheap and easily transportable shelters, which were simple to erect, were needed for the troops who had to spend the winter in the Crimea. Various kinds of such quarters were developed and manufactured both in England and France. Paxton designed a folding tent and a hut that could be dismantled, and he recruited a thousand of the skilled workmen who had been working on the Crystal Palace at Sydenham. Formed into a special building squad, they were sent to the Crimea.

The greenhouses offered by Cranston's of Birmingham were also made of wood with smooth panes of glass which did not have to be fitted with putty, but were kept in place by special knobs. The buildings were ventilated by flaps in the plinth on which the glass panes were laid. These buildings parts could be used with a variety of groundplans which made an architect superfluous.

In the United States too there were, by the middle of the nineteenth century, manufacturers of prefabricated greenhouses such as Woodward and Hitchings. They had plenty of well-to-do customers, especially around New York. In a catalogue of 1865, 'Woodward's Graperies', a range of glasshouses with wooden frames, was offered, amongst them long lean-to greenhouses with arched roofs suitable for growing vines. The firm of Hitchings, later Lord & Burnham, also used only wooden structures to begin with.

The first glasshouse with an iron frame was erected in 1881 by Lord & Burnham at Lyndhurst in New York state, the country house of the railway magnate Jay Gould. Today Lyndhurst belongs to the National Trust for Historic Preservation. The original frame of the glasshouses is now being restored and has been painted its original chrome-yellow. What was unusual was that an architect was employed, presumably at the request of the owner of the building, and the design was produced in conjunction with the New York office of Pugin & Walter.

Leafing through the old catalogues of Lord & Burnham, one comes across many prominent names amongst the owners of sometimes huge complexes of glasshouses and conservatories. Not only Gould, but Rockefeller, Eastman and Colgate were customers of the company. The catalogue shows illustrations of private wintergardens as well as extensive buildings for use in botanical gardens such as the classical conservatory in St. Louis and that in the New York Botanical Garden in the Bronx (pages 106–9).

Though these buildings had iron frames, their structure and architectural details are firmly fixed in the tradition of the nineteenth century.

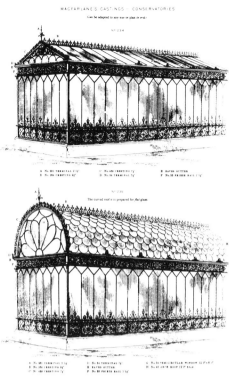

Conservatory from the catalogue of Walter MacFarlane & Co. of 1882.

The Great Palm Houses and Public Wintergardens

'Some of these gardens have winding walks, fountains, and even plots of grass and ponds of water, so that the only difference between them and the real garden is, that glass intervenes between the summit of their trees and the sky; and nothing can be more delightful when there is frost and snow upon the ground outside, than to enjoy the genial warmth and verdant beauty within.'

John Claudius Loudon[31]

With Paxton's building at Chatsworth an important era in the history of modern glasshouses came to an end. In his conservatory of 1836–41 he had created the first large-scale interior which was lit by daylight. The effect on his contemporaries of such a huge enclosed space where the light came from all around must have been enormous, for this was something quite new to the people of the nineteenth century.

Loudon's and Paxton's buildings largely established the pattern of glasshouse building of the future. Early glasshouses had been relatively small. Even Rohault's extensive complex in the *Jardin des Plantes* in Paris (1833) did not possess a very large continuous interior. The characteristic of public glasshouses built in the forties and after Paxton was their great size.

Though the interior of Rohault's building was not so large, his was the first extensive complex of glasshouses for a botanical garden which was constructed entirely of iron and glass.

P. F. Suys' building for the Royal Horticultural Society in Brussels (1826–30), though very large, was, because of its structure and severely classical appearance, a direct descendant of the orangery.

While the planthouses in Kassel and at Syon House, built like orangeries, met their owners' requirement for grandiose buildings, the use of a feudal style for the Brussels building was in direct contradiction to its function, for this was a building for the general public.

Charles Rohault de Fleury (1801–75) was the son of the well-known Parisian architect Hubert Rohault de Fleury. After finishing his studies at the Ecole Polytechnique he devoted himself to sculpture before settling down as an architect in 1825. His first project was the *Passage du Saumon*, which he designed in collaboration with his father. During the rebuilding of Paris under Napoleon III, Rohault chiefly designed residential buildings. Together with Henri Blondel he designed the buildings around the Place de l'Opéra, but was not successful in the competition for the Opera itself.

When Rohault was given the commission to design the new glasshouses for the Natural History Museum in the Jardin des Plantes in Paris, he went to England with one of the professors of the Institute to gather information. At Loddiges Nurseries he saw glasshouses built after Loudon's designs.

His own designs show how stimulating he found this visit. In the detailed records of the buildings he designed for the Jardin des Plantes (among which there was also a small monkey house), he left a full description of the buildings he had seen in England.

Rohault's designs were for a complex of about 180 m divided into two halves. The two taller central structures, one of which was intended to hold palms, were divided by a ramp. An arch over the groundfloor made a visual link between the two symmet-

Glasshouses in the Jardin des Plantes, Paris (1833–4), Charles Rohault de Fleury.

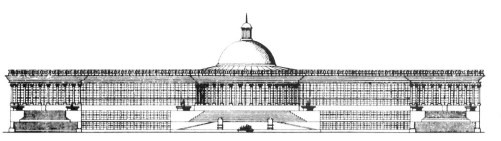

Glasshouses in the Brussels Botanic Garden (1826–30), P. F. Suys.

rical parts. The glasshouses which were glazed on three sides backed on to a massive building to the north which contained the heating installations and stairwells.

But the building was only completed up to the right central building (pages 62–3). The second wing was never built.

The following decade saw the construction of a number of large glasshouses in England and France. This advance was led in England by Richard Turner (1798–1881) and Decimus Burton (1800–81).

Decimus Burton, the son of a building contractor, had the traditional education of an architect, followed by a journey to Greece. As early as 1821 he designed one of the terraces for Nash's Regent's Park, and his subsequent buildings were all characterised by the classicism of the time.

Richard Turner, on the other hand, was an engineer as well as a designer. His Hammersmith Iron Works in Dublin supplied the prefabricated iron building components for the wintergarden in Regent's Park and the palm house at Kew.

The palm house in the Botanical Gardens in Belfast (1839) was the first building with which Turner's name was connected but he was only the builder: the palm house was designed by Charles Lanyon. The palm house in Dublin, on the other hand, was designed and built by Turner in 1842, and this became a prototype for his subsequent buildings.

The glasshouses in Belfast and Dublin, as well as Burton and Turner's palm house at Kew, are all in botanical gardens. Their aim was above all scientific, but they were open to the public from the first. This had not been the case for any length of time. Kew Gardens, which belonged to the royal family, was closed to the general public until 1841. Palm houses now began to have a dual purpose, for as well as their scientific (and therefore educational) objective, they now became public wintergardens.

Early glasshouses had also been used in this way, but they had always been privately owned or were only open to the members of the horticultural society to which they belonged.

The earliest public wintergarden mentioned in the literature on the subject was in Berlin. The description of the *Teichmann'sche Wintergarten* in the *Encyclopaedia* may have been written during Loudon's first visit to Europe in 1813–14. Loudon, who considered the Berlin wintergarden the first of its kind, saw others in Strasbourg, Potsdam and Vienna.

The plants in the Berlin wintergarden (the description of it is of a traditional orangery) were mainly oranges and myrtles. The trunks of the trees grew out of the middle of round tables.

The building was mainly used as a social meeting-place. 'It is almost needless to say that in these gardens or orangeries there are plenty of seats and small movable tables; there are also, generally, bands of music, a reciter of poetry, a reader, a lecturer or some other person or party to supply vocal or intellectual entertainment; and short plays have even been acted on the Sundays. In the evening the whole is illuminated, and on certain days of the week the music and illuminations are on a grander scale than ordinary. In some of these orangeries there are separate saloons, with billiard tables for ladies who object to the smoke of tobacco, also for card-playing and for select parties. If you enter these gardens in the early part of the morning, during the winter season, you will find gentlemen reading the newspapers, taking chocolate, and talking politics; after three o'clock you will see ladies and gentlemen, and people of every description, sitting among the trees, talking or reading, and smoking; or with punch, grog, coffee, beer, or wine before them. In the saloons, you will see those gentlemen and ladies who cannot bear tobacco; which, however, in some orangeries, is not allowed, and in others is only permitted till a certain time in the day. When the audience leave the theatre in the evening, a great number of well-dressed people, of both sexes, are in the habit of visiting these gardens before they go home, to see the beauty of the vegetation when brilliantly illuminated by artificial light, and to talk of the play and the players.'[32]

While this early example of a wintergarden held plants which had been typical of planthouses of the eighteenth century, the glasshouses of the forties were filled with exotic plants.

In 1846 the wintergarden of the Royal Botanic Society was opened in Regent's Park in London. Decimus Burton had originally been asked to design it. His first proposal was for a structure which was to be predominantly of wood, his second for a

Wintergarden in Regent's Park, London (1846), Decimus Burton and Richard Turner.

building with a 'ridge and furrow' roof on an iron framework. Of the manufacturers who were asked for estimates, that of Turner's Hammersmith Iron Works was the most attractive. During the cooperation between architect and engineer which followed, Turner evidently greatly influenced the structure of the building.

At first only part of the building was put up, and it was thirty years before the construction was completed. It was not until 1871 that the east wing was added, and the west wing was built five years later.

A description of 1850 runs as follows: 'The wintergarden stands upon an area of 15 000 square feet [ca. 1400 m²]. It is 100 ft across the widest part, and 175 ft in length. It forms a portion only of the original design, and was built by Mr. Richard Turner, of Dublin. It consists wholly of glass and iron, without walls or brickwork of any kind appearing above ground; being therefore an extremely light and elegant structure, admitting light on all sides. . . In form this building consists of a series of five span-roofs placed against each other, running south and north, and one in front running east and west. . . Ample ventilation is provided by movable sashes, which are opened and shut simultaneously in each roof by means of machinery. The upright glass of the front and back can be opened freely in the way of French windows or folding doors.[33]

The walls were divided by small split pilasters framing a space filled with red and blue glass. The curve of the roof running straight down to the walls, and the wings ending in semi-spherical apses, created a most elegant overall effect.

The proposed additions envisaged space for a lecture hall, a library and a museum. Though the members' interest was chiefly in the botanical aspect of the plant collection, the plants were laid out decoratively rather than scientifically. The trees and shrubs grew in irregular groups to produce the impression of a landscape. Visitors could leave the wintergarden through any of the doors which opened on all sides and come in again at a different place.

This building therefore also served several purposes. It was both a planthouse and a social meeting place. Unfortunately it does not exist any more but was demolished in the 1930s.

At about the same time as the wintergarden in Regent's Park, the Great Palm House in the Royal Botanic Gardens at Kew was built (pages 68–73). It was opened in 1848.

Here too it was Burton who was first asked to provide a design. Independent of him, Turner put forward a proposal of his own and provided a detailed cost estimate at the same time. When the building was finally planned, a synthesis of these designs was used. It is difficult to say whose was the larger share in the final design, but the fact

that the form of the structure was dictated wholly by consideration of the building's function and the necessary stability, without any ornamentation to its plainness, is presumably due to the influence of Turner, the engineer.

Burton, who at first wanted to enhance the building with architectural features borrowed from masonry constructions, found it difficult to forego his role of architect in buildings of this type. This is especially noticeable in another planthouse which he designed on his own in 1859 and which was built near the palm house (pages 78–81).

Unlike Burton, whose building enterprises lay mostly in quite another field, the construction of glasshouses was Turner's speciality. He offered to an expanding market private conservatories, designed by himself, of a type which showed characteristics of the buildings at Kew and in Regent's Park, and he also constructed functional buildings like the second train shed at Lime Street Station in Liverpool. For the competition for the Crystal Palace he submitted a design for a huge vaulted hall which was to be built of prefabricated iron parts. This design, unlike his earlier buildings, included decorative features not essential to the structure. Although, as we have seen already, Paxton received the commission, Turner and his French colleague Hector Horeau received a 'special mention' for their designs, the only ones of the 245 submissions to do so.

Burton and Turner are a good example of the professional differences between architect and engineer. There had been no such occupational division in earlier centuries, but with the necessity for scientifically exact calculations of structural forces, without which the new buildings could not be erected, the new profession of construction engineer arose. His predecessor had been the engineer-corps officer or military builder of the eighteenth century who was responsible for building fortifications, bridges and roads. With the foundation by Napoleon of the Ecole Polytechnique education in France was also split, for the engineers studied at the Ecole Polytechnique, while the architects went to the Ecole des Beaux Arts.

The different problems of construction reflected the differing views of the profession. While the architects felt committed to the Fine Arts, the engineers, unencumbered by tradition, were only concerned in carrying out their task efficiently.

Nowadays there is a tendency to look on the buildings put up by engineers as the 'authentic' (Gloag) architecture of the nineteenth century, and to consider these the men who prepared the way for modern architecture. Though the last century did not completely deny the beauty of many structures erected by engineers, this does not mean that artistic intentions should be attributed to them. This would have contradicted

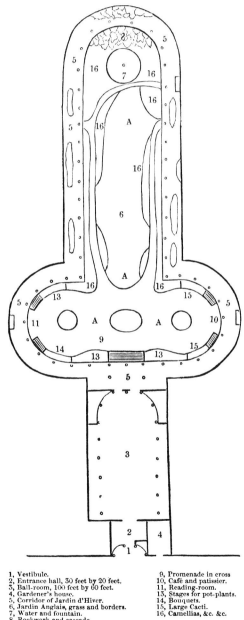

1, Vestibule.
2, Entrance hall, 30 feet by 20 feet.
3, Ball-room, 100 feet by 60 feet.
4, Gardener's house.
5, Corridor of Jardin d'Hiver.
6, Jardin Anglais, grass and borders.
7, Water and fountain.
8, Rockwork and cascade.
9, Promenade in cross
10, Café and patissier.
11, Reading-room.
13, Stages for pot-plants.
14, Bouquets.
15, Large Cacti.
16, Camellias, &c. &c.

A. Jardin d'Hiver; extreme length, 300 feet; extreme breadth 180 feet; extreme height 60 feet.

(*Gard. Chron.*, for 1848, p. 70.)

Jardin d'Hiver, Paris (1847), H. Meynadier and M. Rigolet.

their own view of themselves, for they would have agreed that a building only became a work of art with the help of an architect.

At about the same time as the two buildings in England which were discussed above, two large public wintergardens were built in France, one in Paris and the other in Lyons. Unfortunately neither is still standing. The purpose of these buildings was not botanical but commercial. Real estate companies and building speculators were quick to recognise the needs of the public and, with their wintergardens, created fashionable meeting-places.

The *Jardin d'Hiver* in Paris was built in 1847 from a design by H. Meynadier and M. Rigolet. It stood in the newly laid-out Champs Elysées, between the avenue Montaigne and the rue Marbeuf. An earlier, smaller wintergarden, built in 1846, had not found favour with the Parisian public because of its small area and lack of height, and was demolished after only six months. The new building was conceived on a more generous scale, apart from an extensive garden it contained a ballroom, a café, a reading room and living-quarters for the gardeners.

In 1848 the *Gardener's Chronicle*, which was published by Loudon, printed the following description: 'Upon leaving this [the ballroom] you at once enter the corridor, or lower gallery, of the Jardin d'Hiver, or, as it looks at first, fairy land, so grand, lofty and tasteful, light and elegant does the whole appear. From this corridor you look down upon the garden which is in the form of a cross, 300 feet long and 180 feet wide. Towards the farther end you see the 'Jardin Anglais', about 150 feet long, laid down in grass, intersected with borders containing large shrubs and trees, among which rises a noble *Araucaria excelsa* from the Jardin des Plantes. . . about 50 feet high; beyond you see a cascade and fountain playing nearly to the top of the building, and the whole terminated by rockwork; at the sides of the cross on the corridor are arranged noble orange trees, and below you, thousands of camellias and other plants; the corridor or lower gallery extends round the interior of the entire building, and is about 15 or 20 feet wide. The roof, which is exceedingly light and elegant, is constructed of iron, and supported by more than one hundred iron pillars in a double row resting upon the corridor.[34]

The corridor or lower gallery mentioned is presumably a walkway on the ground floor and not the gallery suspended below the roof on which one could not walk, but which held dwarf palms and rhododendron bushes. The actual garden seems to have been slightly sunken.

Both ends of the building and the side walls of the transept were covered with mirrors. Steam heating kept the building at a comfortable, steady temperature, even on the coldest winter day.

We find the same groundplan of a main aisle and transept in Paxton's Crystal Palace. An earlier wintergarden, built by Thomas Hopper in 1811 for Carlton House in London, had an even more specifically ecclesiastical groundplan. It consisted not only of a main and two side aisles, but its iron framework imitated a gothic structure.[35] The Paris wintergarden did not stay up for long. Under the laconic headline 'Wintergarden demolished', the *Moniteur des Architectes* published, in 1860, a view from above and a section of the building.[36]

At the same time as the Paris *Jardin d'Hiver* (1847) the wintergarden in Lyons was built. Its groundplan was square, and there was a raised inner gallery from which visitors could enjoy a fine view of the whole area with its trees, shrubs and flowers.

The design was by Hector Horeau (1801–72), an architect who left a great number of remarkable designs which were never carried out. Some of them were, indeed, impossible to build. Almost all his projects showed his adherence to modern methods of construction and materials such as iron and glass. His designs were mostly for exhibition buildings, market halls, hotels, barracks, office buildings, footbridges and arcades. In the 1860s he designed various projects for the Paris boulevards, combining the concept of an arcade with that of a wintergarden. Enormous glass roofs spanned the street, plants hung from iron structures and grew up pillars. In 1871 he designed an office building for the space where the old Paris Opera was located. It was a structure of glass and iron with a glassed-in courtyard. Lifts were attached to its facade. A design of the same year for a Paris city hall was based on the same principle. A perspective drawing of the building, with part of it cut away, shows a tree-lined inner courtyard which could be seen from the windows of the various floors around it, and which would have been covered by a vaulted glass roof.[37]

The 'Crystal Art Palace' in Glasgow (pages 82–9) was opened in 1873.

This too reflected the new role of the planthouse, for while the motive for raising exotic plants in earlier glasshouses was an interest in botany, here the plants were merely used as a decorative and symbolic background. The main concern had become 'to produce beautiful surroundings, pleasant to be in.'[38]

The purpose of the 'Crystal Art Palace', designed and financed privately by John Kibble, corresponded very closely with the trend of the time which reached its height in the 1870s.

Architecturally, on the other hand, it belonged to a past era, for the clean lines of the first half of the century were not in demand any more.

Jardin d'Hiver, Paris (1847), H. Meynadier and M. Rigolet.

While it was mostly England and France who pointed the way with their iron and glass buildings, and Germany did not begin to build iron structures until later, it is worth looking at some of the German glasshouses. Most of these buildings do not exist any more, for many, like the planthouses in Hanover-Herrenhausen, were destroyed in the raids of the Second World War.

Though German architects were familiar with the English and French iron structures through the architectural journals, traditional building materials rather than iron were used in many instances when iron would have been suitable. When the Frankfurt opera house was built in 1880, the idea of an iron roof truss was rejected on account of its cost. Yet concealed iron structures had been used as a matter of course in comparable buildings, like the Paris Opera, which was built some ten to fifteen years before, and the Royal Albert Hall.

Germany also remained far behind England and France in the construction of bridges and railway stations. The first important railway bridges were not built until the middle of the century, a time when the English railway network was already fully developed. Testing and standardisation of materials did not become general in Germany until the 1870s, and until that occurred it was impossible for the manufacturers of iron building components to compete against traditional building materials.

The palm house built in the Berggarten at Herrenhausen by the architect G. L. F. Laves in 1846–9 demonstrates clearly that only its cost stopped iron from being used. The rectangular wooden columns of the facade were faced with cast-iron half-columns, presumably to simulate the English and French iron columns.

Heinrich Hübsch (1795–1863), who was court architect at Karlsruhe, used wood to construct the glasshouses and wintergardens he built in 1853–7 at the Baden Residence. When the buildings were remodelled, the wooden structure, which was found to have rotted after only ten years, was replaced by an iron one.

The whole complex, consisting of a series of buildings where glass buildings and stone buildings originally alternated, was based on traditional architectural concepts. The wintergarden is of special interest since its iron framework was only covered with glass in the winter.

In Germany the majority of large glasshouses was built after the 1860s. They were mostly found in the botanic gardens of Berlin, Karlsruhe, Munich, Schönbrunn, Strasbourg and Würzburg. The glasshouses in Stuttgart (pages 64–7) and Kassel (pages 52–4) are two of the few important early examples. The building at Kassel, which is not a pure iron and glass structure, belongs to the category of traditional buildings derived from the orangery.

The palm house at Herrenhausen designed by Laves burned down in 1879 and was replaced by a building of iron and glass designed by Auhagen. This building was taller than any of its predecessors (ca. 30 m in height), but its unassuming architecture could not bear comparison with any of the English buildings.

As in most other German glasshouses, only straight surfaces, rectangular groundplans and span roofs were used in this building. There were about thirty-four glasshouses in the Berggarten in Hanover in 1850, the first having been built in 1755. Unfortunately none of the early buildings has survived.

Palm house in the Berlin Botanic Garden (1857), Herter and Nietz.

The buildings which were erected one after the other in the botanic gardens in Berlin could serve as an example of the gradual development of German glasshouses, for the Körner building of 1907 is the first revolutionary contribution to the complex which began to catch up with the level of international glasshouse construction.

The botanic gardens which are now at Berlin-Dahlem were, until 1897, on the site of the present-day Kleist park at Schöneberg. The Berlin botanic gardens were founded by the Great Elector (Frederick William of Brandenburg) and became the court apothecary gardens under Frederick William I, administrated at that time by the *Societät der Wissenschaft* (Society of Sciences). The gardens were further enlarged by Frederick II but became dilapidated during the Seven Years War. They were not reconstructed until a cabinet decision of 1801 taken chiefly for economic reasons, for the gardens were to be used for research into those pigment-producing herbs which were important for the textile industry. The botanic gardens became part of the university at this time. The gardens were enlarged in 1891 to include a central botanical department for the colonies which was financed by the government. This department was given the task of researching the fundamental principles of raising tropical plants which could be of economic and culinary use. During an earlier time of expansion the building plans were in the hands of the state's chief architect, Schinkel. When, in 1819–20, it was decided to build new planthouses, amongst others a palm house, Schinkel recommended that a 'rotunda constructed of rafters' should be built 'in such a way that a chimney, in the form of a pillar in the middle of the building, should serve both as an ornament and a support'. But this suggestion was not used. A wintergarden, said to have been built in 1820 by Schramm after a design by Schinkel, is mentioned in *Berlin und seine Bauten* ('Berlin and its Buildings'). When this book was published in 1896, the wintergarden was evidently still standing.

When, in 1821, a building was required to house palms and a dragon tree, Schinkel again suggested a rotunda. This was to be built with straight rafters. 'The whole back of the conical building to be covered and lined with zinc, and only the front glazed.'

The design was carried out, but the building was demolished in 1832, since the wooden ribs had rotted. It is not clear from existing sources what the building looked like, since it is sometimes called a hemisphere[39] and sometimes conical[40]. Since straight rafters are mentioned in the design, the unusual conical shape is the more likely. The hemisphere may refer to the first proposal.

Schinkel may have found the inspiration for his designs in Loudon's buildings, for the structure resembled the half-domes built against a north wall which Loudon recommended. Loudon's *Encyclopaedia* did not appear in a German translation until 1823, but Schinkel probably read English books and publications on the subject.

Schinkel ceased subsequently to be connected with the buildings for the botanic gardens, and nothing more came of his designs.

When Schinkel's palm house was demolished in 1832, the plants were put into other glasshouses. Some went into the palm house on the Pfaueninsel, a glasshouse which had also been designed by Schinkel, assisted by his pupil Albert Dietrich Schadow in 1829–31 (page 39).

A replacement for the old palm house was not opened until 1859. This building, which also does not exist any more, was designed by Herter and Nietz and shows no English influence at all. It was made up of three rectangular buildings of green glass, with

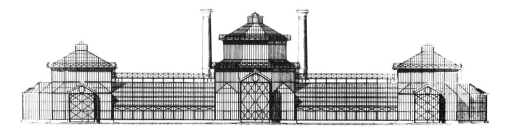

Glasshouse in Strasbourg (1877–82), H. Eggert.

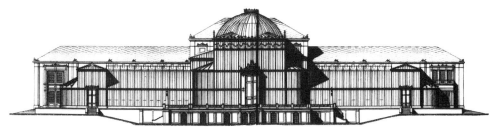

Glasshouse in the Munich Botanic Gardens (1860–65), August von Voit.

the central structure taller than the others. The glass roof was made up of individual long span-roofs. A large building containing offices and living-quarters was attached to the back of the palm house which was a building of glass and iron, 17.4 m high and of a total length of 54 m.

This building was architecturally more like exhibition halls, such as the Munich crystal palace, than typical planthouses. The author of an article in the *Zeitschrift für praktische Baukunst* ('Journal of Practical Architecture') wrote that a 'modest elegance' could not be denied the building, but that it was doubtful whether it could be thought 'the equal of the crystal palaces of Kew Gardens and Herrenhausen'.[41]

Though many architects studied the English buildings on the spot before designing their own, the curved roof did not become popular in Germany. Only the building in the Würzburg botanic gardens, which was constructed before 1860 and which is unique, has a long, unbroken glass front with a vaulted glass roof sloping from the roof-ridge towards a lower stone building lying to the north. The architect of the palm house at Schönbrunn in Vienna also used curved surfaces for the roof. But this building, which was obviously influenced by the English glasshouses at Kew, is not as elegant as the buildings it was based on. The skylights set in the vaulted roof spoiled the overall design.

The novelty of this Viennese building lay in the way the framework and sashes were on the outside with the glass skin attached inside, a principle of construction which was also used by Körner in his great glasshouse of 1907 in Berlin. But the palm house at Schönbrunn lacked the formal economy of Burton and Turner's palm houses. (Though an article in a German architectural magazine of 1887 said of the palm house at Kew that the exterior did not produce a happy effect.[42])

There were practical reasons for the preference for flat roof surfaces to curved roofs. It was easier to roll the slatted wooden screens which were used for shade over flat glass panes. Curved glass panes were also more expensive to manufacture, as was pointed out by H. Eggert, the architect of the glasshouses built in 1877–82 for what was then the Kaiser-Wilhelm University at Strasbourg.

Looking at the Strasbourg building one is struck by the way the architect made no effort at all to hide the chimneys, but placed them quite unashamedly to the left and right of the central pavilion. It was evidently thought unnecessary to produce a grandiose structure such as August von Voit (1801–70) tried to achieve with his design for a conservatory in the botanic gardens at Munich.

August von Voit, who had designed the Munich crystal palace in 1854, tried to give his conservatory an architectural character, probably to make it fit in with the museum building to which it was attached. While the crystal palace was a very down-to-earth structure, much influenced by the London building, Voit tried, not very successfully, to raise the tone of the conservatory by adding extraneous architectural decorations. Putting span roofs side by side with domes and conical roofs gave the exterior a lack of clarity and did not do away with the stiffness of the building.

When the botanic gardens in Nymphenburg were remodelled and reopened in 1914, there was no need for Voit's conservatory any more, and it was demolished.

From the 'Functional' to the 'Architectural' Glasshouse

If we look at the dates of the construction of the various glasshouses chronologically, we can see two phases in their development before the middle of the nineteenth century.

The first phase began in 1815 with Mackenzie and Loudon's designs for glasshouses with curvilinear outer skins and ended with Paxton's Great Conservatory at Chatsworth of 1836. Most of these early buildings were of relatively modest dimensions and simple groundplan, rectangular, circular or elliptical.

The second phase, which began in the 1840s, produced large public glasshouses which were distinguished by ground plans composed of several rooms running into each other. These separate areas varied in height. Almost all these buildings were based on the original principles of the structures which had pioneered such glass buildings. They had glass roofs with iron ribs almost to the ground, which let in the greatest possible amount of light. They gave up all claims to traditional architectural ideas, and neither building elements nor materials were concealed. This phase lasted until the beginning of the fifties and was the time when the great glasshouses in London, Lyons and Paris were built.

In the middle of the century iron became so fashionable that the Ecclesiological Society asked the architect R. C. Carpenter to design an iron church.[43] The first cast-iron churches were also shipped to the British colonies at this time. After this phase had reached its culmination with the Crystal Palace in 1851, 'architectural' glasshouses became more numerous, though there were exeptions as, for example, Kibble Palace. The Temperate House in Kew Gardens (pages 78–81), begun in 1859 and designed by Decimus Burton, shows the change in trend. The building, which was erected without the assistance of Richard Turner, appears very traditional compared with the palm house which was built fifteen years earlier.

The monumental complex is made up of a central building, two octagonal pavilions and two wings. The stepped, glazed, tent-shaped roof starts from a masonry wall with windows and square, protruding pillars. The main entrance is in a porch which is richly ornamented with stucco and crowned by statues and vases in classical style. This presents a great contrast with the unpretentious doorways of the palm house. Though the Temperate House may constitute a retrograde step from the point of view of the building's purpose, one cannot help being fascinated by it. With its suggestion of far-eastern temple roofs it seems to promise a fairy palace rather than a planthouse.

The palm house in the Botanic Garden in Edinburgh (pages 76–7), also belongs to the architectural planthouses. This sandstone building in the classical style, which appears monumental because of its height, lets in little light through its windows which are separated by broad columns. The glass roof which rests on the cornice has the same section as Burton and Turner's palm house at Kew. Despite the glass roof, it is fairly dark inside, but it was obviously decided that this was worth it for the sake of the grandiose exterior.

The trends in architecture as a whole are, of course, reflected in the design of glasshouses, where changing fashions and preferences for various styles appear.

The popularity of the new materials, iron and glass, was also subject to changes of taste. With the spread of the gothic revival and the anti-industrial craft movement, the new building materials were pushed into the background.

John Ruskin, an influential theoretician of the backwards looking gothic revival, rejected all use of iron in architecture. The new building material was damned as a symbol of industrialisation, and it also ran counter to a historically faithful use of gothic forms. Other critics disapproved of iron for its lack of a plastic, sculptural effect and a 'violation of the aesthetic sense'.[44] The apparent fragility of the structures led to a feeling of insecurity for those who, used to the tradition of stone buildings, equated stability with mass.

This change, a trend which appeared not only in architecture, had become apparent for some time.

Technical and economic developments had altered the living conditions of all classes of society in a very short time. The population explosion and the migration of the rural population to the towns had led to an enormous expansion of the towns and the creation of the modern cities. Many traditions had been destroyed. Craft had fallen victim to industry. The belief in social and technical progress which had begun in the age of enlightenment, now mingled with anxiety and pessimism about the future, and the sharpening social conflicts only added to these problems.

An answer to this disquiet seemed to lie in an emphasis on traditional cultural continuity. Religious revival movements and the enthusiasm of the romantics for the middle ages ran parallel with the emergence of the gothic revival. The social utopians Ruskin and Morris believed that the misery of the industrial society could be relieved by a revival of the production methods of medieval crafts as in the early craft guilds.

The artists and architects of the Arts and Crafts Movement tried to set the individually made object against the hated anonymity of manufactured products. They failed to see that crafts could not supply the needs of a mass society. Instead of making use of the new technology, Morris and other artists produced handmade objects for the home, which were only within the reach of the well-to-do.

The inability to come to terms with the present manifested itself architecturally in an antithesis between innovative, technical solutions and, at the same time, a return to the styles of the past.

A classicism which sprang straight from Greek and Roman antiquity developed in the middle of the eighteenth century, a time when archaeology became an accepted science. The increasing volume of archaeological literature which followed, often written by practising architects, constantly offered new models for 'archaeological' styles. The spread of classicism took a certain level of education for granted, not only among architects, but also amongst the general public. Many architects were able, thanks to their scholarship and large vocabulary of styles, to produce both classical and gothic designs.

Historicism, in the sense of a complete pluralism of architectural fashion, incorporating a wide choice of exotic styles, appeared for the first time in the nineteenth century. It led in the course of the century to an eclectic use of a variety of styles, even on one and the same building.

The dichotomy between the client's and the architect's attitude to the new building materials led to the well-known combinations of 'functional' structures and historical architecture. Railway stations of iron and glass, built purely to be practical and stable, had a building attached to them to give them a traditional facade. Doubts about the new achievements and an inability to produce a new style showed itself in a wish to bring back the past. The engineer's functional building was not thought beautiful and was considered to need cosmetic treatment by an architect.

Most architects nevertheless felt the lack of a specific style, and this search for a 'new style' dominated discussions until the middle of the century. The question, 'In which style should we build?'[45] showed in which direction the architects were looking. They hoped that by turning to the past a style would emerge which could be used in their own time.

The camellia house in the park of Wollaton Hall near Nottingham (pages 58–9) was built at a time (1823) when classicism was still the predominant style. Though the building was outwardly traditional, quite unorthodox materials and construction methods were used. The whole facade with its Tuscan columns is built of prefabricated cast-iron components.

The gothic conservatory at Carlton House belongs to the same period. But the gothic style, which was only considered suitable for garden pavilions and private houses, was at that time not thought of as a serious rival of classicism. The planthouses in Kassel at Syon House and Alton Towers belong to this classical tradition. But at this time there were also some pioneering buildings which, forgoing all traditional styles, consisted only of a framework covered by a glass skin. These functional structures appear astonishingly 'modern' for their time.

The concept of functionalism as a specific programme among architects and craftsmen did not, of course, exist at this time, though the connection between form and function was already beginning to be suggested. This concept was heralded by a demand that the building's form should be appropriate to its use, that suitable materials should be employed and that the structure itself should be seen rather than hidden. This 'pre-functionalism'[46] of the first half of the century belonged to the era when the classical style was predominant, and ended when it fell from favour. For classicism, with its formal restraint and its predilection for bare surfaces, came closest to the aesthetic of functionalism.

The demands of the new building technology continued to be met within the tradition of classicism and had little effect on prevailing building practices. The development towards twentieth century functionalism did not begin until the end of the nineteenth century.

This trend can be seen in early glasshouses as well as in other structures built for a special purpose. Some remarks by J. C. Loudon also point in that direction, though

Residence with 'gothic' greenhouse, from *The Greenhouse Companion.*

36

Palm house on the Pfaueninsel, Berlin (1830–31),
Karl Friedrich Schinkel and
Albert Dietrich Schadow.

Palm house on the Pfaueninsel, Berlin. Painting by
Karl Blechen (1832).

they are strangely at odds with other statements by this man who, with his textbook for architects and builders, the *Encyclopaedia of Cottage, Farm and Villa Architecture and Furniture* (1833), wielded a decisive influence on the taste of his time, and therefore contributed greatly to the popularity of various styles.

Loudon considered that the construction of glasshouses (and with these he meant chiefly his own spherical glass structures) had been improved because their design was no longer left to architects whose competence he questioned in his *Encyclopaedia of Gardening*.

He suggested that the reason why architects showed 'very little taste' in this field was the absence of classical models that they could imitate. Also, architects did not completely understand the purpose of a glasshouse, and he continued his attack on his colleagues, '. . . we are persuaded that there are very few persons who call themselves architects who really understand what constitutes art'.[47]

'To civil architecture, as far as respects mechanical and chemical principles, or the laws of the strength and durability of materials, they [i. e. the greenhouses] are certainly subject, in common with every description of edifice; but in respect to the principles of design or beauty, the foundation of which we consider, in works of utility at least, to be "fitness for the end in view", they are no more subject to the rules of civil architecture than is a ship or a fortress; for these forms and combinations of forms, and that composition of solids and openings which are very fitting and beautiful in a habitation for man or domestic animals, are by no means fitting, and consequently not beautiful, in a habitation for plants. Such, however, is the force of habit and professional bias, that it is not easy to convince architects of this truth; for structures for plants are considered by them no further beautiful than as displaying not only something of architectural forms, but even of opaque materials. Fitness for the end in view, we repeat, is the basis of all beauty in works of use, and, therefore, the taste of architects, so applied, may safely be pronounced as radically wrong.'[48]

It was not so very long before the people constructing such buildings were no longer architects, and those who wanted such structures erected were no longer dependent on architects. For as early as the 1820s such companies as W. & D. Bailey and Jones & Clark specialised in the construction of glasshouses.

Loudon advised anyone wishing nevertheless to employ an architect to suggest to the architect that he consult with the gardener. As a dire warning he quoted the example of 'a conservatory recently erected from the design of one of the most popular and extensively employed architects of the day, in which the interior columns supporting the roof have capital ornaments with leaves of sheet copper, coloured green in imitation of those of a palm.'[49]

Loudon disapproved of this aping of nature. It is possible that he alluded to John Nash who had used such palm columns in the kitchen of the Royal Pavilion in Brighton in 1818–21.

In another book, the *Greenhouse Companion* published in 1824, he argued in favour of harmonising the style of the conservatory with that of the house as long as this did not interfere with letting in plenty of light: '. . . where a house is characterised by some particular style of architecture, it is easy to impress that style on the greenhouse. The form of the heads of the doors and windows, peculiar to the different orders of Gothic architecture, can readily be imitated in the front sashes and doors of a green-house.'[50] The columns of the facade could also be made to fit in with any kind of style. This had already been done at Wollaton Hall.

This contradiction is typical not only of Loudon, but of almost all his contemporaries. They were enthusiastic about Paxton's Crystal Palace, yet expected orthodox solutions to be used for traditional building problems. Paxton and Loudon themselves did not find a new building method for ordinary houses, and their structures were indistinguishable from those of their colleagues.

The change in taste in the 1850s can in fact be seen in Paxton's later designs for iron structures. For even he was not immune to the fashion of the time, with its predilection for exuberant ornamentation and its love of shapes of a historical character.

The objects shown at the International Exhibition in the Crystal Palace were, incidentally, in complete contrast with the architecture of the building itself. Many of the articles exhibited for the Victorian home surpassed themselves in the absurd disguises of their real purpose and furnish perfect examples of what we know as 'bad taste'.

The new opportunities and new aesthetic concepts which lay hidden in railway stations, exhibition halls and glasshouses, were neither fully exploited during the nineteenth century, nor was their importance realised. Even Loudon's call for a building to suit its purpose was confined to functional buildings. That these principles could also be used in other spheres of construction and design was something of which architects were only dimly aware.

There was nevertheless already a premonition that the construction potential of iron might form the basis of the new style after which people hankered. In a lecture in 1846, Karl Bötticher, who taught at the Berlin building academy, predicted that the new style, 'in which a different static principle would form the key-note, would wrest itself from the womb of time'. And that the basis 'of this building method of the future' would be iron.[51]

But with the establishment of historicism, all these progressive tendencies of the early nineteenth century were submerged for a long time. Exposed iron structures were shunned and hidden behind ornate architecture. A good example of this is Garnier's neo-baroque Paris Opera. Wherever the structure was unconcealed, it either copied traditional models or was overloaded with random ornamentation. Iron construction was only rehabilitated at the time of the Paris Exhibition of 1889 through Dutert's *Galerie des Machines* and the Eiffel tower, though by the time of the exhibition of 1900, buildings were again overloaded with decorations, and taste was once more on the rebound.

Flight into Exoticism

Though the middle class became the ruling, and economically the most important class in the nineteenth century, the nobility still commanded great fortunes and large estates and continued to set the tone. In the years of industrial expansion in Germany, the Second Empire in France, and the late Victorian era in England, upper-class ostentation attempted to outdo the feudal way of life.

The palaces and country seats of the European monarchs and nobility possessed not only the most important gardens but also the most magnificent private wintergardens and conservatories.

That some wealthy middle-class people were also able to afford comparatively 're-gal' glasshouses is shown by the Kibble Palace in Glasgow, the palm house in the Golden Gate Park in San Francisco and the glasshouses which belonged to the railway magnate Jay Gould at Lyndhurst near Tarry-town in New York State.

Compared with many of the later winter-gardens, the Duke of Devonshire's Great Conservatory at Chatsworth was relatively unpretentious. Superfluous ornamentation would have run counter to the restraint which was the hallmark of the prevailing classical taste.

But where ostentation and self-glorifica-tion were of primary importance, it was im-possible to be content with a plain building erected by engineers. As far back as the eighteenth century, the orangery, the plant-house of the time, was built for purposes of prestige. The wintergarden of the Royal Palace of Charlottenburg, the wintergarden on the Pfaueninsel near Berlin, that of the Austrian Emperor in Vienna as well as Leopold II's complex at Laeken (pages 90–7), were built in this courtly tradition. Except for the latter, the construction of the buildings was conventional like that of Laves' planthouse at Herrenhausen.

The building materials were wood and stone. Iron was only used fairly late in Ger-many and Austria, one of the reasons being that the iron industry was not sufficiently developed. The building at Kassel is an early exception.

The palm house on the Pfaueninsel in Ber-lin which was built in 1830–1, and the 'Moor-ish' planthouse in the Wilhelma in Stuttgart of 1843 (pages 64–7) belong to the tradition of exoticism that had appeared in the gar-dens of the eighteenth century. The light-hearted use of exotic and historical styles was at first only employed for garden build-ings, and even there classicism was still pre-dominant, but in the 1870s exotic styles were caught up in the maelstrom of indiscriminate eclecticism.

The building on the Pfaueninsel in Berlin had been designed by Schinkel and his stu-dent Schadow for Frederick William II. It was built of wood and glass against a back wall of masonry. A glass onion-dome rose above the central part. The palm house acquired its exotic touch from parts of a Bengali pagoda which was built into it. The building burned down in 1880.

But it was in the interiors of many winter-gardens that exoticism was rampant.

When Ludwig II's living quarters in the Munich royal palace were enlarged in 1867, a wintergarden was included in the plans. This was to be a glass-covered roof garden of enormous size, 200 m long and with a span of 30 m. It took four years to build. Except for the architect, Karl von Effner, and Ludwig's servants, hardly anyone ever saw the interior of this building which was demolished soon after the kings' death.

The functional style of this structure must have been in strange contrast with the interior furnishings which reflected the eccentric taste of the Bavarian king, as well as, in an exaggerated manner, the taste of the well-to-do middle class of the time.

'The young Ludwig II made something colossal of his roof-garden. The western part of the north facade of the palace was spanned by an enormous glass roof, and a garden was laid out so big that there was space for a pond large enough for Ludwig to row on, as well as a brook, fountain, trees, a reed hut and an oriental pavilion. Birds flew about in this paradise of tropical plants and a painting in the background gave the illusion of a further vista beyond this Indian fairytale garden.'[52]

The painting mentioned was a panorama of the Himalayas, the pavilion was made of bamboo and silk, the rowing boats were little 'boats which appeared to be pulled by swans'.[53]

There was also a grotto with stalactites and a waterfall. A special lighting system made it possible to make the interior appear plunged in moonlight or to create a sunset mood.

The Indoor Jungle

While the plants in the early glasshouses were arranged according to a botanical principle, a desire to create an illusion of scenery later took its place. This led to an attempt either to hide the structure of the buildings or to construct them in historical styles.

In botanical gardens like Kew it was axiomatic that '... the plants in the greenhouses and stoves have been thrown into natural groups, so that the principles of classification may now be studied in the plant-houses as well as in the open air'.[54]

The various methods of exhibiting pot plants in glasshouses that Loudon described all have one thing in common, a desire to create the best possible conditions for the plants.

But most of the wintergardens described in this chapter were intended more for aesthetic enjoyment than for those interested in botany.

Under the heading, 'The Picturesque in the Construction of Glasshouses', M. Neumann, Director of the botanic gardens in Paris, gave, in 1852, an excellent description of the principles of these wintergardens.

'What aim should those whose task it is to construct a glasshouse for exhibiting tropical plants keep in mind? It is to imitate the rich disorder of a virgin forest by artistically concealing all obvious traces of artifice, and if possible hiding all material evidence that one is walking under a glass roof. Why indeed should the geometrically regular network or grid of the windows not be replaced by a more or less faithful imitation of the natural forms of branches and boughs, thus letting the light fall through this irregular tracery as it would through the dome of a natural forest? Interweaving tropical climbing plants in these artificial branches complete the picturesque illusion, for they hide the naked metal framework under their foliage and attach themselves in graceful garlands to the swaying branches of the larger trees .... A small brook should wind through a carefully chosen glade, alive with tropical fish, then rush cascading between rocks, to spread out finally in a wide calm basin surrounded by sand and gravel.... One element would still be missing to complete such a scene — the presence of tropical butterflies. One may well exclaim in sceptical admiration at such a concept, but we are not afraid of expressing the opinion that the introduction of these brilliant lepidoptera, though difficult, is not impossible....'[55]

When one remembers Loudon's suggestion that men of various exotic races, if possible from the countries of origin of the plants exhibited, should be employed as gardeners, using them at the same time for educational purposes, Neumann's suggestion will hardly make us 'exclaim'.

Loudon's idea, first expressed in his book *Remarks on the Construction of Hothouses* published in 1817, was not new. In the allegorical gardens of the eighteenth century which suggested remote regions of the world or bygone ages, this illusion was often completed by putting servants into appropriate costumes.

A contemporary illustration of the gardens of Monceau shows servants in exotic costumes leading a dromedary through the park for the entertainment of the ladies and gentlemen. A Tartar tent has been erected under the trees in the background.

The concealment of the structure to create an illusion, such as Neumann suggests, was at least partly realised in Prince Potemkin's wintergarden at the Palace of Taurida near St. Petersburg. The supporting pillars were in the shape of palms, an idea which may have come from Nash's Royal Pavilion in Brighton.

A contemporary description (1827) of the St. Petersburg wintergarden runs as follows: 'As, from the size of the roof, it could not be supported without pillars they are disguised under the form of palm trees. The heat is maintained by concealed flues placed in the walls and pillars, and even under the earth leaden pipes are arranged, incessantly filled with boiling water. The walks of this garden meander under flowery hedges and fruit-bearing shrubs, winding over little hills, and producing, at every step, fresh occasions of surprise. The eye of the beholder, when weary of the luxuriant variety of the vegetable world, finds recreation in contemplating some exquisite production of art: here the head from the chisel of a Grecian sculptor invites the admiration; there a motley collection of curious fish, in crystal vases suddenly fixes our attention. We presently quit these objects in order to go into a grotto of looking-glass, which gives a multiplied reflection of all these wonders, or to indulge our astonishment at the most extraordinary mixture of colours in the faces of an obelisk of mirrors. The genial warmth, the fragrance of the nobler plants, and the voluptuous stillness that prevails in this enchanted spot, lull the fancy into sweet romantic dreams.'[56]

These stage-sets of a private paradise fulfilled the growing desire of the nineteenth century for make-believe and self-deception which was also expressed in the 'panoramas'. Special buildings were constructed in the cities to hold these large circular pictures which showed historical events and scenes from foreign countries. In the 1860s there were six such panoramas in Berlin alone, one of them a 'Panorama of the German Colonies'. In these 'places of a complete imitation of nature' (Walter Benjamin)[57] the city dweller, tired of civilisation, could, after paying an entrance fee, abandon himself to exotic fantasies.

A love of everything exotic which was also reflected in the furnishings of middle-class houses and apartments, was one of the many indications of the rejection of social reality which seems to have been a symptom of the industrial revolution. Conjuring up the past in architecture, literature and painting was also such a symptom.

Like the retreat into privacy, the escape into an artificial paradise or historical situation was a reaction against the radical changes of the present.

The emergence of modern exoticism is closely connected with the great voyages of discovery which brought reports of other parts of the world to Europe. Early exoticism, on the other hand, was still largely a mixture of the pleasure in discovery and a naive delight in everything strange and mysterious. The seventeenth century Dutch 'Chambers of Art and Mystery' were also an expression of this need. In these privately owned forerunners of the present-day ethnological museums, all sorts of strange and curious objects, brought from the colonies by the merchant ships, were assembled.

The feature sections of the newly created 'illustrated papers' produced a new genre of literature in the nineteenth century, stimulating the imagination.

Life in the overseas colonies, especially those of the British Empire, supplied writers with new and exciting material. A 'colonial literature' for those who remained at home began to develop.

Tourism, which translated these desires into reality, was also an invention of the time. By 1869 people could book journeys to Egypt and Palestine at Thomas Cook's travel bureau which had been founded in 1845.

When the French painter Paul Gauguin put an end to his middle-class existence by first becoming a Bohemian and then emigrating to the South Seas, he really only translated into action what his contemporaries dreamed of. The *'Europamüde'* (a person tired of Europe)[58] imagined life in the South Sea islands not only as an ideal of a pre-industrial idyll, but also a life free of social and moral constraints.

Gauguin's contemporaries who did not want to do without the amenities of civilization, could create a synthetic replica of their fantasies in their homes. The conservatory, which could be included in the architecture of a house, became the centre of exotic interior decoration.

The trend increased in the course of the century and reached its peak in the last quarter. Ludwig II's architecture and the literature of the so-called decadence exemplify the aesthetic philosophy of those who had escaped into a solitary world away from society.

In this world even nature could only be enjoyed in an artificial form. Des Esseintes, the hero of Huysmans' novel *A Rebours* (*Against the Grain*) only enjoys those flowers which, because they are exotic, appear quite artificial.

In Emile Zola's novel *La Curée* (*The Kill*), published in 1871, the key scenes take place in the conservatory of a villa belonging to a wealthy building speculator. His wife Renée meets her lover in this conservatory. In the florid descriptions of the conservatory, Zola uses the unrestrained growth of the tropical plants with their heavy, intoxicating scent as a metaphor for the uninhibited sexuality of the actors, moral constraint surrendered before the backdrop of an artificial paradise.

The palm, obvious symbol and cliché of exotic longing, became an indispensable part of the middle-class home.

The furniture and decorations in the studio of the painter Hans Makart represent the taste of many of his contemporaries. Here too there was a palm, part, like the rest of the decorative objects, of a private stage set. Whether the antique objects were authentic was, as in the theatre, of no importance, since their task was merely to create a historical or exotic illusion. This illusion induced a feeling of well-being, for it was now possible to play any part denied by reality.

Such an interior represented '... the universe for the individual. Here he gathered together distant places and the historical past.'[59]

The garden had always been such a microcosm, the wintergarden of the nineteenth century now became a version adapted to city life.

John Claudius Loudon's house, Bayswater, London (1824).

Maison Hallet, 346 avenue Louise, Brussels (1902–5), Victor Horta.

Conservatory of a house at Chesham Place, London.

The Domestic Conservatory

'They came to the last drawingroom, and the conservatory opened out before them, a large wintergarden full of tall trees from tropical countries sheltering massed groups of rare flowers. Stepping under that dark vegetation, where the light slipped through the leaves like a silver shower, one breathed the tepid freshness of the damp earth and a heavy perfume wafting across. It was a strange, sweet, sickly and delightful sensation of artificial nature, enervating and indolent. One walked across carpets like moss between solid masses of shrubs. Suddenly Du Roy noticed on his left, under a large dome of palms, a huge white marble basin, where one could well have bathed, and on its rim four large swans of Delft faience, out of whose half-open beaks water flowed.

'The bottom of the basin was powdered with gold dust, and in it swam enormous red fish, bizarre Chinese monsters with protuberant eyes and blue-bordered scales, like mandarins of the waves, which reminded one, ranging and hovering suspended above this golden depth, of the strange embroideries of that distant country.

'The journalist stood still, his heart beating fast. He said to himself, "This, this is true luxury. These are the houses in which one should live".'

Guy de Maupassant, *Bel Ami*[60]

While the great planthouses of Syon House, Chatsworth and Wollaton Hall stood at some distance from the living quarters, the conservatories which, from the 1860s, became an indispensable part of an English or French middle-class house, were mostly built on to existing buildings. For one thing there was not enough space in the gardens of the towns and suburbs for a separate building, and the use of the conservatory to enlarge the house became also more important than a burning interest in botany and the well-being of the plants. Attaching the conservatory to the house also had the advantage that no added heating was required.

A series of articles were published in the *Revue Générale de l'Architecture* of 1855 dealing with the conservatories which were becoming the fashion at the time.[61] The author emphasized right away that this was a new and lucrative sphere of activity for the architect. Since the article was addressed to a middle-class market, he began with the simplest and cheapest examples, special windows for displaying plants, and small glasshouses for balconies. Since the cost of glass and iron had greatly decreased, a small conservatory, he suggested, was within the reach of everybody.

The glasshouses which were available in England, and which were assembled from prefabricated parts, had already made it

possible for the most modest houseowner to build on a glasshouse at no great cost and without difficulties. The various building systems made it possible to acquire conservatories conforming to special measurements, according to a desired groundplan and financial capability.

Probably the earliest example of such a conservatory can still be seen in the house in Bayswater which Loudon built to his own design in 1824. The conservatory of this semi-detached house had access from both it and its neighbour and could be seen into from the front rooms. The roof was a dome covered in glass scales.

Loudon's conservatory did not look out of place as many later examples did, but fitted smoothly into the architectural whole, since half of it was part of the projecting roofed veranda, using the same vertical structure and ledges.

The problem was solved in a somewhat similar manner when Victor Horta designed a house with a conservatory for Max Hallet in Brussels. This conservatory was built on to the back of the house and was made of three circular sections and glass domes one above the other. It was attached to the first floor of the house, and this created the illusion that it might fall off at any moment.

But the typical groundplan of an attached conservatory was rectangular, half of an oval, or semi-circular. Where a gallery with access to several rooms was required, a long conservatory was built. While the transition from the house proper to the conservatory which had been built on later was made quite easily indoors by covering the floor with the same material in the adjacent room and decorating it with plants, most of the conservatories in the contemporary architectural journals look out of place from the outside, since the glass buildings are so different from the rest of the architecture.

In a contemporary article on a conservatory attached to a house in the boulevard Arago in Paris (ca. 1885), the writer takes pains to point out that the architect was not content to employ prefabricated iron components, but used his 'artistic talent' to design all the sections himself and then had them made up from his designs. When one compares this building with others constructed of standardised parts, like those offered by Walter MacFarlane of Glasgow, one wonders whether such expenditure was justified.

In the English journal *The Builder* a conservatory extension was illustrated in 1895 which still exists today, though not in its original form.[62]

Among the somewhat monotonous city buildings, this addition looks like an exotic excrescence, with the difference in scale of the windows of the conservatory and the house appearing particularly strange. The

Conservatory of a house on the boulevard Arago, Paris.

WINTER · GARDEN · IN · THE · ANGLO · JAPANESE · STYLE   CONSTRUCTED · ON · THE · PATENT · SYSTEM · OF · MESSENGER · & · COMPANY · HORTICULTURAL · BUILDERS · LOUGHBOROUGH · 1880   FROM SKETCHES BY E.W. GODWIN, F.S.A.

owner had planned for the plants to act as a decorative background for a group of sculptures which were placed in the livingroom in front of the conservatory's glass partition. The metal dome was presumably originally covered in glass and was surmounted by a lantern.

Whether the conservatory was attached to the drawingroom, diningroom or library, one could always see into it from the adjacent room. This allowed one to look into greenery when the view into the open was blocked.

Conservatories were usually built on to the southern side of the house, on the ground-floor or on a terrace. Conservatories on the roof were rare. The largest of such glazed roofgardens was Ludwig II's which has already been described. A large store which sold plants owned a conservatory on the roof of a town house of several storeys in London. Charles Fowler, the architect of the planthouses at Syon House, designed a roof conservatory for the upper terrace of Covent Garden market in 1827. There is also a very beautiful glasshouse on Otto Wagner's *Ankerhaus* in Vienna (1895). But this structure, evidently based on planthouse designs, was not used as a conservatory but as a photographic studio.

The Viennese group of architects, Haus-Rucker & Co., has recently made the glazed roofgarden topical again. A catalogue published in 1973 encourages New York apartment owners to create such 'rooftop oases'.[63] A quite fantastical illustration shows a conservatory on the roof of an apartment house. A transatlantic offspring of one of the side wings of the palm house at Kew sits, curled into a semi-circle, like a glass snail on the roof.

Most of the prefabricated glasshouses reflected the taste of the late nineteenth century and were built in a mixture of styles with a variety of ornamentation. The manufacturers made full use of the fact that cast-iron was easily cast in any shape. This enabled the middle-class customers inclined to pretentiousness to choose anything from 'Anglo-Japanese' to Moorish conservatories when ordering their building.

It did not matter that the buildings did not really do justice to the styles they vaguely suggested. The customer's idea of Japanese or Moorish architecture was probably equally confused. Such lapses of taste would have been inconceivable during the classical period at the beginning of the nineteenth century, when both owners and architects were too well informed to allow such caricatures of style.

After Japanese art had been shown for the first time at the International Exhibition in London of 1862, European painters and architects began to show great interest in all things Japanese. Monet, Van Gogh, Whistler and others were enthusiastic about Japanese woodcuts. Japanese interior decoration became fashionable.

It is therefore not surprising that amongst the designs commissioned by the glasshouse manufacturers Messenger & Co. from the architects Godwin and Adams there was an 'Anglo-Japanese' conservatory. These designs for Messenger & Co.'s catalogue of 1880 showed the various ways in which the standardized parts could be assembled. Godwin, who designed wallpaper, furniture and interiors in Anglo-Japanese style had, as far back as the 1860s, emptied his house of western furniture and 'furnished' it in Japanese style.

The catalogue contained designs for special windows in which plants could be kept, glazed verandas and free-standing glasshouses. There were also conservatories which were attached to the house and could serve as entrance halls or lobbies. A two-storeyed glasshouse could be connected with the main house by a glassed-in bridge at first-floor level.

The elegant design of these buildings, which claimed to be 'artistic conservatories', was especially stressed. It would probably never have occurred to Loudon to make such claims for his glasshouses.

The ornaments and decorations of these buildings could hardly be reconciled with the Japanese models from which they were allegedly copied. The extravagance of style was mostly used to differentiate one type of conservatory from another, so as to maintain the manufacturers' hold on the market.

The variety in the choice of styles appeared to increase with the growing wealth of the middle classes who could afford any kind of conservatory and wanted to show this off for all to see.

Hotel Wintergardens and Wintergardens in Health Resorts and Spas

The nineteenth century hotels, as well as the spas and health resorts, provided new opportunities for wintergardens to be built to add to the facilities for leisure and recreation. Every kind of eclecticism flourished in the French spas of Vichy, Vittel and Evian, where splendid and varied architecture supplied a backdrop against which spa-life was carried on. Special types of resort buildings, like pump-rooms and covered walks evolved.

Glass and iron were the most suitable materials for this purpose, and these buildings resembled the wintergarden not only in their outward appearance but in their function. For the pump-rooms and covered walks were 'out of doors' yet protected from the weather. Charles Garnier, the architect of the Paris Opera, built the thermal baths at Vittel in 1883–4. A hall with an interior gallery was connected with the other buildings by an iron covered walk. The hall which was glazed was, of course, decorated with palms.[64]

The assembly rooms at Göggingen near Augsburg even included a palm house which was also used as an 'open-air theatre'.[65]

Until the beginning of this century, not one of the great hotels from Berlin to Monte-Carlo was built without a wintergarden. These wintergardens were usually connected to the diningroom, as for example at the Central-Hotel in Berlin, at the Frankfurter Hof, and at the Schweizer Hof in Lucerne where the diningroom itself had a glass roof. A beautiful example of a diningroom with a glass roof can still be seen in the former Palace Hotel (now Sheraton) in San Francisco. But the plants only played a minor role in

Wintergarden of an English sanatorium.

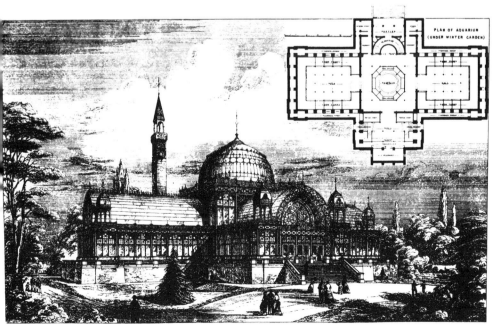

Wintergarden and aquarium at Llandudno around 1875.

all these buildings. The wintergardens were used as public rooms.

The Central-Hotel near the Friedrichstrasse station in Berlin opened in 1880 and its wintergarden met a general need. 'Kroll's Garden', built in 1844, had ballrooms and a restaurant, and had also included glazed wintergardens in the side wings, but the care of the plants had been too much trouble, and the plants were moved and the glass roof demolished.[66]

The intention of the builder of the Central-Hotel was 'to create a large concert and restaurant complex which would offer an area like a garden, full of greenery at all times of the year, well lit and rather like the Paris *café-concerts*'.[67]

The wintergarden, which was enclosed by the hotel on three sides, covered an area of almost 75 m in length and over 20 m in width. Three thousand people were able to eat there and in the adjacent restaurant at one time. The height to the ridge of the glass roof was almost 18 m, the wintergarden was therefore almost as tall as the palm house at Kew. Instead of a gallery, theatre boxes were built into the sides, and from these one could look down into the hall.

The building was designed by the Berlin architects von der Hude and Hennicke, who had already designed the Hotel Kaiserhof.

The 'Winterpalace' – Eclecticism and Business

'...the desire by the private owners to create an effect with their buildings tended to lower the standard of private architecture in comparison with that of public buildings.'[68]

The Paris *Jardin d'Hiver* was one of the earliest examples of a wintergarden to which public rooms had been added, though the main focus still lay on the garden, since the appeal of exotic plants was still new and attracted the public.

For a long time the wintergardens in Lyons and Paris remained the only ones of their kind. When the speculators discovered this type of building after 1860, there was a full-blown boom in such multi-purpose buildings, not only in the big cities like Cologne, Frankfurt, Berlin, Leipzig, London, Dublin and Paris, but also in English seaside resorts.

Here the focus had plainly shifted. The wintergarden itself was only one of a variety of attractions offered.

Since 1854 there had been a *Jardin d'Acclimatation* in the Bois de Boulogne in Paris, a mixture of zoo, botanic garden and amusement park. Here the *Palais d'Hiver*, a descendant of the long-demolished *Jardin d'Hiver* was opened in 1891. More than half the building was taken up by a planthouse and 'palmarium' which led into a big hall. The roof of the wintergarden consisted of six parallel vaulted glass roofs of short spans. The palm house lay in the taller main building which has an architectural facade.

Since the power to attract crowds had evidently gone out of the word 'wintergarden', 'palace' was added as a fitting superlative both in Paris and in Dublin.

Similar buildings, erected in the seventies in English seaside resorts like Brighton, Scarborough, Torquay, Great Yarmouth, Llandudno and Hastings were called an 'Aquarium'. But they were not merely devoted to fish in tanks, for the aquarium itself took up only a small part of the building.

Assembly rooms and palm house in the Frankfurt Botanic Garden (1878), H. T. Schmidt.

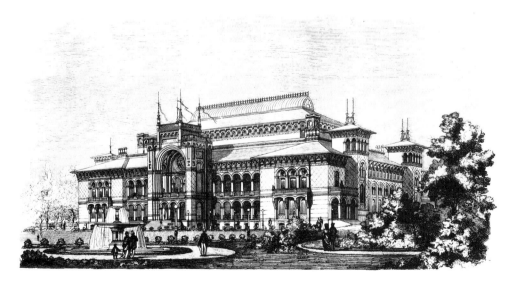

Flora, Berlin-Charlottenburg (1871–4).

In an article on the 'Royal Aquarium' in Westminster, the writer says: 'Aquaria, winter gardens, floral halls and skating rinks appear to be the popular resorts of the day, and have opened a new field for speculative companies and a novel source of work to the architect.'[69] Skating rink and wintergarden were found under one roof as well as clubrooms, concert halls and restaurants.

Joint-stock companies were the backers of these enterprises and arcades too.

Most of the buildings mentioned were built during the golden age of eclecticism and historicism. The public was presented with styles called Moorish, Italian, Renaissance and even 'Swiss-Gothic', most of them a mish-mash of imaginary styles.

Architecture became an advertisement for the enterprise behind it. Borrowed styles from foreign cultures or from the past promised a wonderful fairyland which would carry off the visitor, leaving everyday life behind, into another reality, even if only into the mysterious underwater world of the aquaria.

One of the earliest examples of this new building style in Germany, which was discussed in the *Handbuch der Architektur* ('Handbook of Architecture') under the heading 'Public Places of Amusement and Festival Halls', stands in the Frankfurt botanic garden.

The building, which was finished in 1871, was largely destroyed by fire seven years later. A competition for a design for a replacement was immediately announced. The prizewinning entry by H. T. Schmidt was designed 'in the architectural style of the German renaissance' and was built in only ten months by the building firm of Philipp Holzmann.

From the concert hall and restaurant one could admire the scenery of the palm house through large glass partitions. It was rebuilt after its destruction in the Second World War, and still fulfils its old function.

The 'Flora' in Berlin-Charlottenburg, built in 1871–4, and the assembly rooms and palm house in the Leipzig botanic garden (1900) have the same groundplan as the building in Frankfurt.

In both cases an 'architectural' stone building was combined with a modern steel construction, a principle which was also used in the construction of many railway stations. While the facade of the 'Flora' gave no hint of the iron and glass building which lay behind it, the Leipzig building quite consciously incorporated the vault of the glasshouse in its design. The facade, with its four round towers, thus becomes a peculiar mixture of railway station and castle.

How much the architectural theory of the nineteenth century differed from its practice can be seen in the Charlottenburg 'Flora' which appears to us today as an arbitrary collection of the most diverse styles.

The building, which is presumed to have been based on designs by the architect of neo-gothic churches Johannes Otzen (1839–1911), was built by Hubert Stier (1838–1907). Stier claimed that his building 'created modern architecture on the basis not of one single style taken arbitrarily from the historical development of architecture, but on the basis of the total development ... on the basis, above all, of the two styles which reached the highest and most individual development, gothic and renaissance'.[70]

The 'Flora', which, like many other such buildings, belonged to a commercial company, did not yield the expected profit. The *Handbuch der Architektur* expressed the opinion in 1904 that the enterprise was 'doomed to failure'.[71]

Two late examples of this type of building, a type which fell into oblivion in the twentieth century, are still in existence. They are the People's Palace in Glasgow which was not built for the well-to-do middle classes but for the workers, and the wintergarden of the Casino in Pau in the Pyrenees which was built in 1898.

The stylistic tradition which these buildings shared with the architecture of seaside resorts, music halls and theatres was carried on in the American and English cinema palaces of the twenties and thirties of this century.

Assembly rooms and palm house in the Leipzig Botanic Garden (1900).

People's Palace, Glasgow (1898).

Syon House (England), Conservatory (1820–27)
Design: Charles Fowler

Syon House stands in a large park reaching down to the Thames opposite Kew Gardens in London. Since the sixteenth century it was first the seat of the Dukes of Somerset, then of the Dukes of Northumberland. Here the Duke of Somerset established one of the earliest botanical gardens in England, and it was at Syon House that the botanist William Turner wrote his book *Names of Herbs* in 1548.

In the second half of the eighteenth century the park was transformed into a landscape garden by the famous garden designer 'Capability' Brown who used an existing stream to create a lake more than 350 m long.

The botanical tradition was continued by the third Duke of Northumberland who commissioned the young architect Charles Fowler (1791–1867) to design an extensive planthouse.

Fowler, co-founder of the Institute of British Architects, was already well-known for his numerous market buildings, among them Covent Garden market.

His building in the park of Syon House is in the transitional style between the baroque orangery and the nineteenth century conservatory. Characteristic of this style is the breaking up of the original orangery into a central building, two side wings and corner pavilions. In this it resembles the buildings at Alton Towers (page 17) and Kassel (pages 52–4) which were built around the same time.

Like some of the eighteenth century orangeries, the wings enclose the garden in a semi-circle. This gave the building two fronts, one shielding it from the outside, one opening on to the garden. Fowler tried to

combine two irreconcilable aims: a wish, on the one hand, to allow the greatest possible amount of light into the building, and a desire, on the other hand, to create traditional architecture in stone. The glass dome which rises from the severely structured central building demonstrated the latest technical advances. Loudon's glass dome at Bretton Hall (page 21), which rose direct from the ground, reached approximately the same height.

The transition from circular to square shapes – that is from the spherical dome to the flat surface of the four short saddle-roofs – is made by means of triangular concave areas. The dome itself is carried on an inner arcade of cast-iron columns.

While all pillars and trusses were made of cast-iron, and were presumably designed and cast especially for the conservatory, the ribs of the dome are of wrought iron.

A wooden structure covered with thin metal was later put up over the arcades. Unfortunately this destroys the effect of the loftiness of the interior which is almost 20 m high.

1 Garden view.

49

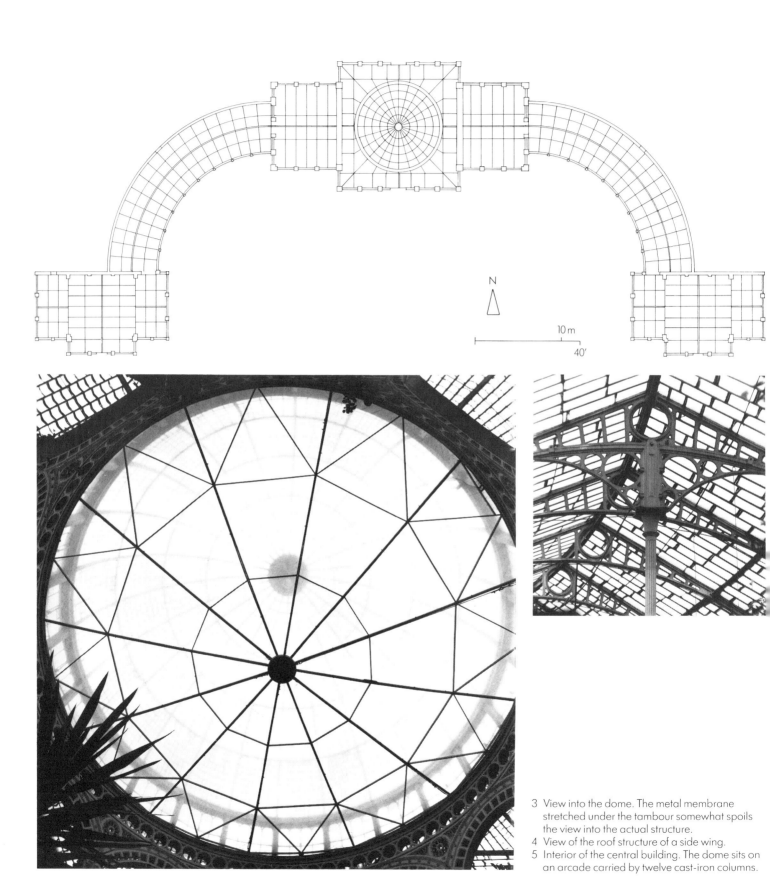

N

10 m

40'

3 View into the dome. The metal membrane
  stretched under the tambour somewhat spoils
  the view into the actual structure.
4 View of the roof structure of a side wing.
5 Interior of the central building. The dome sits on
  an arcade carried by twelve cast-iron columns.

Kassel (Germany) Wilhelmshöhe, Great Conservatory (1822)
Design: Johann Conrad Bromeis

The Great Conservatory on the so-called Bowlinggreen was one of the first building projects of the Elector William II, who came to power in 1821. The new building took the place of a long narrow greenhouse of wood and glass with a diningroom in its central pavilion which was demolished in 1822.

Johann Conrad Bromeis (1788–1855), who had become the Elector's head architect, was in charge of all building projects until the end of William's reign in 1831. He had studied at the Kassel academy at the same time as Georg Ludwig Laves, the architect of the palm house in the Berggarten at Herrenhausen. Only two of his predominantly classical buildings (though he did build a gothic cowshed) are still standing at Wilhelmshöhe, one is the guardhouse (now *Schlosscafé*), and the other the theatre by Leo von Klenze which Bromeis remodelled to make a ballroom.

The design of the conservatory is derived from the baroque orangery, but the glass roofs and the iron and glass dome over the originally round central pavilion were innovations. The building which faces south is walled to the north and on both sides. The original plan was for a facade divided by stone pilasters, but Bromeis used cast-iron columns in the design which was adopted.

He had already used iron columns when he had rebuilt the opera house in 1821, and the Teufelsbrücke (devil's bridge) built in 1826 is made of cast-iron. The use of iron was at this time far from common in Germany. The conservatory's low dome of iron and glass was probably the first of its kind in the country. Technically the building can be compared with the English buildings of the time. Loudon's first glass domes were erected only a few years earlier. It is even possible that Bromeis knew Loudon's first publications. Loudon, in his turn, reproduced the Kassel building in his *Encyclopaedia*, calling it '... a magnificent range of houses...'[72] Loudon's illustration gives a good idea of the original appearance of the conservatory.

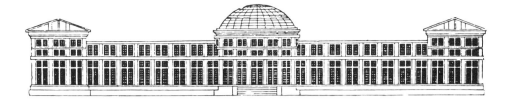

1 Groundplan and elevation of the building in its
original condition from Loudon's
Encyclopaedia of Gardening.
2 General view from the south.

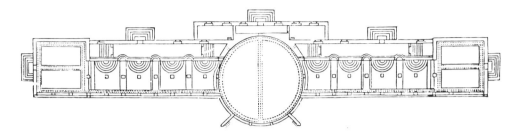

Bromeis was able to use iron only because there was a state iron foundry in Veckerhagen, as well as a state foundry in Kassel and the smaller concern of the Henschel family.

While the firm of Henschel claims in their commemorative pamphlet for their 125th jubilee to have constructed the iron dome and the Teufelsbrücke, the iron foundry at Veckerhagen is named as the manufacturers elsewhere.[73]

The central building of the conservatory was demolished in 1887 and replaced by a palm court, a larger and taller rectangular building with a steel roof.

3 View of the central building.
4 The cast-iron columns in the central building carry a sandstone entablature.
5 View of the roof structure of the central building.

Bicton Gardens (England), Palm House
Designer unknown

Bicton Gardens lies on the south coast of England, near East Budleigh in Devon. The gardens were laid out by the French garden designer Le Nôtre in 1735.

This palm house is one of the most remarkable glass buildings of the nineteenth century. Though smaller than most of the buildings discussed in this book (approximately 21 m in length and barely 10 m at its greatest width), it is of special interest since it is an impressive example of the pioneering phase of iron and glass construction.

Since no plans or documents connected with the building have survived, it is impossible to be certain of its date, architect or builder.

According to Sir George Mackenzie, who in a lecture to the Horticultural Society remarked, 'Make the surface of your greenhouse roof parallel to the vaulted surface of the heavens, or to the plane of the sun's orbit,'[74] Loudon had been experimenting with glass domes and half domes since 1815. Mackenzie and Loudon thought that a curved glass skin would make the best use of light.

In the years which followed, Loudon designed many of his glasshouses with a curved glass skin. All of these were built by W. & D. Bailey of London to whom Loudon made over, in 1818, the rights to his designs, and the use of the curved wrought-iron sash-bar he had developed, for any further buildings. In Loudon's *Greenhouse Companion* and his *Encyclopaedia of Cottage, Farm and Villa Architecture and Furniture* several of these designs are illustrated (pages 19f).

The similarity, down to the smallest detail, of these designs with the palm house at Bicton, allows us to conclude that this building was based on a design by Loudon, and that it was put up by Bailey's. Since the palm house is marked on a map of 1838, the building was presumably erected between 1818 and 1838.[75]

The palm house belongs in the category of 'lean-to' glasshouses, since it is built against a wall which shields it to the north. A second, lower building was often built against the other side of a north wall and used as heating room and toolshed. At Bicton the stone wall follows the curve of the glasshouse and only juts out slightly beyond it. It holds some of the ventilating flaps, while others are in the roof-ridge.

Loudon's remarks about another of his buildings, the glass dome at Bretton Hall, are also valid for this structure which has only one cast-iron column in two places in the interior: 'It is worthy of remark, that there were no rafters or principal ribs for strengthening the roof besides the common wrought-iron sash-bar...'[76]

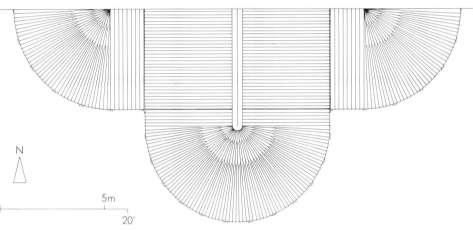

N

5m

20'

1 Front view.
2 Plan of the roof.

The number of ribs decreased towards the roof-ridge, two ribs running into one. In this way the distance, and therefore the width, of the glass scales remain the same.

The building only became stable when the panes of glass had been fitted.

This building is covered in small glass panes fitted like fish scales in the same way as the conservatory in Loudon's house in Bayswater which is still standing. This type of glazing, which ceased to be used later, made it possible to glaze a curved surface with straight glass panes. Larger panes would have had to be curved. But a more important reason was probably that the tax on window glass was not lifted until 1845. Since the glass manufacturers were taxed on the weight of the glass, but had to charge their customers by its surface area, the manufacturers tried to produce the thinnest possible glass which was very fragile when used in large panes. The solution was therefore to use small panes held by many thin ribs.

3 View upwards into the roof structure. Ventilation
  flaps are in the back wall and the roof-ridge.
4 View at an angle.
5 Side view. The palm house is built against a
  wall sheltering it from the north, which follows
  the line of the roof.

Wollaton Hall (England), Camellia House (1823)

Designer unknown

This glasshouse, which does not at first sight seem unusual, stands in the park of Wollaton Hall near Nottingham. Wollaton Hall itself can be seen in the background of the illustration.

The irregular, polygonal groundplan of the building is due to the fact that the building's back wall was built against the wall of an already existing higher terrace.

The building was conceived for the particular needs of camellias. The camellia house was a cold greenhouse which, according to the *Encyclopaedia of Gardening*, should not let in too much light, since an excess of direct sunlight can harm the plants. This explains why only part of the roof is glazed.

The tent-like roofs above the flowerbeds are covered in glass scales, while vaulted metal roofs span the pathways.

The whole roof is carried by slender cast-iron columns which lead the rainwater into gullies under the paths. There the water comes into contact with the pipes which carry the hot-water heating, so that when the heating is on, the water is vaporized. This provides the necessary humidity in addition to the heat which rises through the iron gratings.

This building is unusual not only because its roof is of iron but also because the whole classical facade was constructed of prefabricated cast-iron parts. This may well be one of the earliest examples of a completely prefabricated iron building.

It is not, on the other hand, an example of modular production, but was manufactured as a one-off design. As well as cast-iron, lead was used for the urns on the roof ledge, and copper for the window frames.

While it is now known[77] that the camellia house was manufactured by Jones & Clark of Birmingham in 1823, there is no clear indication who was the architect. Gilbert Herbert suggests that either Jeffrey Wyatville or C.R. Cockerell might have been the designer. Cockerell designed a building which resembles the camellia house at The Grange in Hampshire, and this glasshouse had also been built by Jones & Clark. But the camellia house at Wollaton Hall may have been designed by Jones & Clark themselves, using Cockerell's building as a model.

The photographs show the building in 1978 when restoration had just begun.

1 Detail of the cast-iron facade.
2 General view. Wollaton Hall is in the background.
3 Plan of the roof.
4 Interior. The paths between the beds intersect under the square skylight.

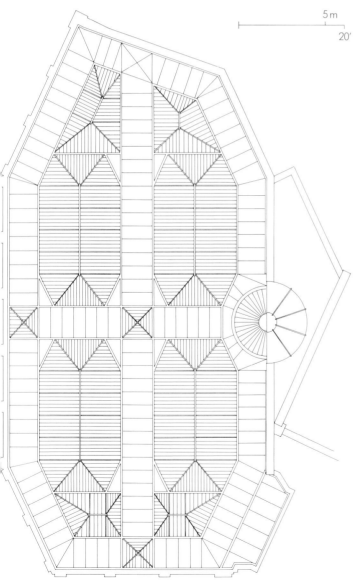

Meise (Belgium), Jardin Botanique National de Belgique, Water Plant House (1854)

Design: Auguste Balat

Balat's small glasshouse had already been moved once, before it was put up in the botanic gardens in Meise. It had originally been built in the zoological gardens in the Parc Léopold in Brussels but was later moved to the botanic gardens in Brussels to house a Victoria Regia. When the botanic gardens were moved to Meise on the edge of Brussels in 1940–41, the Victoria Regia house was also moved.

The supporting structure, with its royal crown on top, stands on an octagonal stone foundation. The trusses are on the outside, presumably to avoid condensation from falling from the cold iron parts.

The restoration of the building was begun in 1978.

1 View of the roof structure with the crown on top.
2 Plan of the roof.
3, 4 Views. The photographs were taken while the building was being restored.

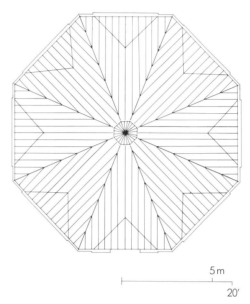

5 m
20'

Paris (France), Jardin des Plantes, Glasshouses (1833-4)
Design: Charles Rohault de Fleury

'Face to face with this spacious, light and graceful building,... with its vigorous vegetation, its many colours visible through its thousands of windows, with its terraces decorated with vases and tropical plants, one imagines oneself transported under oriental skies in the middle of one of those mysterious gardens of which one reads marvellous descriptions in the stories of *The Thousand and One Nights*.'[78]

This building, praised so effusively in a contemporary guide to the Jardin des Plantes, does not exist today in its original form.

But today's complex still reflects Rohault's basic concept, for the steps, terraces and the ramp which rises between the two central pavilions still stand as Rohault designed them, as do the masonry structures built against the slope on the north side which contain the heating system, gardeners' living quarters etc. The eastern wing, which would have made the building symmetrical, was planned by the architect but never executed. A wintergarden was erected in its place in 1882, and this was demolished in 1932 to make room for a new building. The western wing, with its two long curved roofs set one above the other, consisted originally of two quarter-vaults. The central pavilions still have the proportions of Rohault's design, but instead of the straight surfaces of the old hipped roof, the present-day roof is curved and supported by curved steel trusses.

Rohault left very complete documentation of his buildings in the Jardin des Plantes. The volume of *Das Naturhistorische Museum in Paris* ('The Natural History Museum in Paris'), published in 1837 in both French and German, contains groundplans and views of the glasshouses, animal houses and museum buildings, as well as several detailed drawings of the cast-iron building parts used in the construction. He prefaces the discussion of his own designs with a section about the English glasshouses which he had seen on his stay in England as a student in 1833. The curved glass roofs of the wings in his design are modelled on the English buildings.

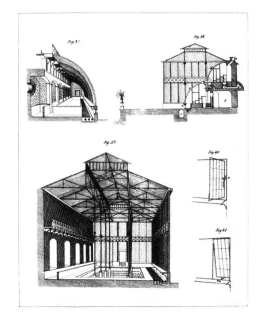

1 Sections through the original side wings and central pavilions.
2, 3 Groundplan and elevation from Rohault's book.
4 Side view of the eastern and central pavilions.
5 General view from the south-west. The terraces, stairs and ramp are still in their original condition.

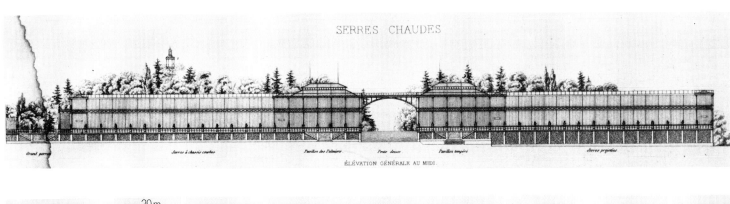

SERRES CHAUDES

ÉLÉVATION GÉNÉRALE AU MIDI.

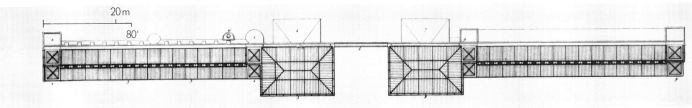

20 m
80'

Stuttgart (Germany), Bad Cannstatt, Wilhelma, 'Summerhouse with Living Quarters and Ornamental Plant Houses in the Moorish Style' (1842–6)
Design: Karl Ludwig Wilhelm von Zanth

'This villa, conceived in the style of the country seats of the Italian nobility, consists of a house surrounded by plant houses, colonnades, pavilions, gazebos, a ballroom, theatre and servants quarters. They stand in grounds where flowerbeds, basins, fountains and plantations of trees alternate in a regular pattern. The whole forms the outermost part of the royal park of Rosenstein ...'[79]

The construction of this complex, which is called after the Württemberg king William I for whom it was built, took more than ten years. It was designed as early as 1829. The building which was later described as a 'Moorish country house' was originally intended for a 'bath house' since mineral springs had been found in the adjacent Rosenstein Park.

The planning and style of the building had largely been dictated by the royal client. 'Instructions were laid down that the house should be connected with ornamental plant houses and that a Moorish style should be employed' (Zanth). It was not until the country house and the glasshouses were already being built that the king commissioned his architect to create the complex which has been described above. The fashion for exotic styles was not new (page 16). There had been buildings in Moorish style in the gardens of the eighteenth century, such as the mosque which still stands in the park at Schwetzingen and the 'Alhambra' which does not exist any more but which was one of the many exotic buildings that Sir William Chambers had designed for Kew Gardens.

But while a Moorish building stood beside a Chinese pagoda and a Greek temple at Kew, the Wilhelma buildings are all in the same style. The small structures at Kew were also merely used as pavilions, but the Moorish buildings in the Wilhelma were full-size living quarters and conservatories. William's project is therefore comparable in size with the Indo-Chinese Royal Pavilion at Brighton.

Zanth himself does not seem to have been altogether happy with this Moorish style. He saw in it 'the reign of an untrammelled imagination' rather than 'recognised laws' which he believed could only be found in Greek art.

He therefore set himself the task 'to eschew the aberrations of this kind of architecture without renouncing its advantages which offer tempting, but on the whole capricious, ornamentation ... it was therefore important to affect the imagination strongly by exploiting the exciting characteristics of this architecture without using anything which went against reason and taste'.[80]

This attitude led to a compromise. While Zanth accepted some of the typical elements of Islamic architecture quite literally, such as the horseshoe-shaped arches, the multi-coloured keystones of the window lintels, the chiselled decorations and the dome over the central building which was destroyed in the Second World War, he used them on a building which was fundamentally European in its architectural conception.

The original central building probably came nearest to the king's oriental fantasy. The iron structures of the glasshouses are predominantly plain, and their Moorish elements, like the small scalloped arches on the top windows, really have no proper purpose. It is easier to convey the oriental feeling convincingly in the massive stone buildings than in transparent planthouses for which there is no Moorish model. Though Zanth's buildings did not achieve the imaginative effect of the Royal Pavilion (John Nash, though a classicist, seems to have tackled his task in a much more uninhibited manner), it is difficult not to be captured by the charm of the Wilhelma.

The complex has been restored after being much damaged in the Second World War, and is now almost in its original condition with the exception of the Moorish country house which now has a modern glass roof. The cast-iron glasshouses have been very carefully restored. Their iron parts were manufactured at the iron foundry at Wasseralfingen in 1843–4. Some of the structural parts had to be newly cast, taking the original parts as models.

1 General view from the south-east.
2 Elevation of the building as it was at an earlier time.

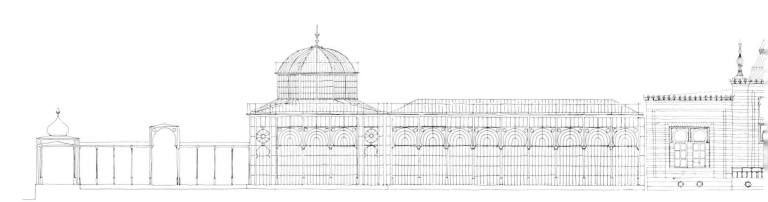

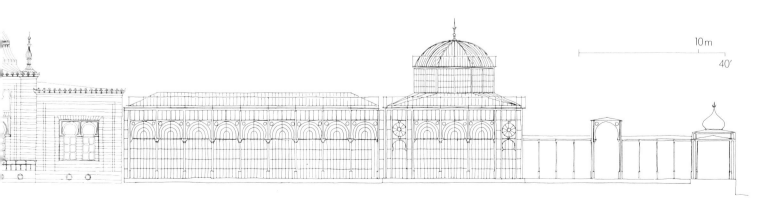

10m
40'

3 View of the roof structure of the fern house.
4 View of the fern house and covered way leading to small pavilion.
5 Interior of the fern house.

Kew (England), Royal Botanic Gardens, Palm House (1844–8)

Design: Decimus Burton and Richard Turner

The Great Palm House at Kew is a synthesis of independent designs by Burton and Turner. The fact that such a building was proposed is partly due to Sir William Hooker, Director of the Botanic Gardens at the time, partly to the fact that Queen Victoria, visiting Chatsworth in 1843, was very impressed by Joseph Paxton's Great Conservatory, which was at that time still the only one of its kind in England.

The cast- and wrought iron structure, not quite 110 m long, is built on a stone plinth one metre high which holds the lower ventilation flaps. Pivoting windows in the upper lantern provide ventilation above. Heat was produced in a subterranean heating system of twelve boilers, which provided hot water for the heating pipes laid under the floor (see groundplan).

The floor itself was made of cast-iron gratings laid over the pipes. Even when the temperature out of doors was below freezing, it was possible to keep the interior of the building at 27° centigrade.

Since one did not want to spoil the appearance of the building by chimneys, a 130 m long subterranean tunnel was built which led to a chimney in the shape of an Italian campanile. This tunnel did not only hold an outlet for the smoke, as at Chatsworth, but also a railway to supply the heating system with fuel. But the smoke outlet never worked perfectly, and later two chimneys were built on to the upper lantern, but these have since been demolished.

The campanile also served as a water tower to provide the necessary pressure for the sprinkling system in the Palm House.

In the central building, which is 20 m high to accommodate the tall palms, a gallery half-way up is reached by two spiral staircases.

The roof-supports are curved sections placed at a distance of 3.75 m, reinforced by tension rods. They lie in cast-iron pipes which serve as distancing bars between the ribs.

The roof was originally glazed in green glass. The glazing of such an enormous surface had become relatively cheap since the

window tax had just been abolished. The total cost, without excavations and tunnel, was £30,000. All iron parts of the structure were manufactured by Turner's own company, the Hammersmith Iron Works in Dublin.

1 View from the east.

2 View from the north-east.
3, 4 Groundplan and section. The groundplan
      shows the heating pipes and grating in the
      floor.
5 Interior looking towards the western entrance.

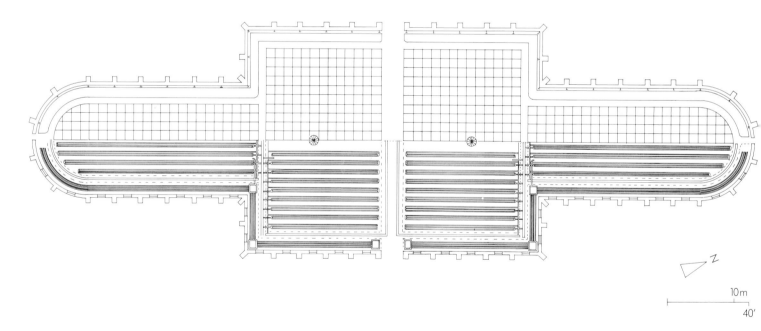

10 m

40'

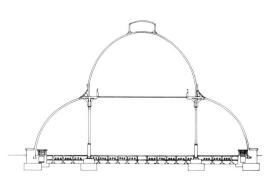

6 Detail of a cast-iron column under the gallery.
7 Interior of the central building seen from the gallery. The railings are decorated with palms, a motif from Greek architecture.
8, 9 Views of the spiral staircase to the gallery.

70 View of the narrow south end.

Chatsworth (England), 'Conservatory Wall' (1848)

Design: Joseph Paxton

Chatsworth, the seat of the Dukes of Devonshire since the seventeenth century, lies in Derbyshire in the English Midlands. Here Joseph Paxton began his career as head gardener to the sixth duke in 1826 (page 22).

Of the many planthouses Paxton built at Chatsworth between 1828 and 1858, the only one still standing is the conservatory wall, and even this is not in its original condition. Before these glass cases were put up there was only a back wall with espaliered trees. In the winter, curtains were drawn over the trees to protect them from the cold. When Paxton built the glasshouses in 1848, this became superfluous.

The conservatory wall is made up of ten pavilions about 2 m deep, and a taller central part. Since there is a difference in height of almost 8 m in the whole length of over 100 m, Paxton divided the buildings like a staircase into individual steps. Inside, there is an ascending pathway.

The structure is made of wood and glass. The roof was originally pleated after the 'ridge and furrow' principle as in Paxton's other glasshouses and rose slightly towards the back wall. The window frames of the facade could be taken out in the summer.

Two rare *camellia reticulata* which Paxton planted in 1850 still bloom in the central building.

1 General view.
2 View of the central pavilion.
3, 4 Groundplan and elevation.

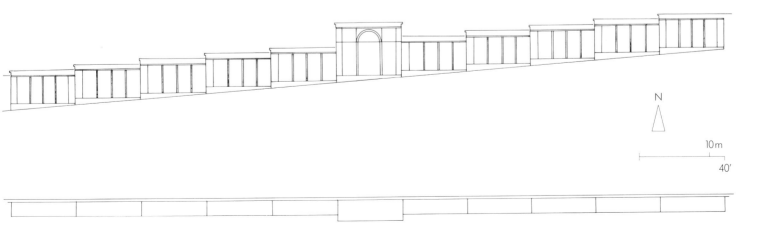

N

10 m

40′

Edinburgh (Scotland), Royal Botanic Garden, Tropical Palm House (1834) and Temperate Palm House (1858)
Design: R. Matheson

The botanic garden in Edinburgh is the second oldest in Great Britain, and, like most botanical gardens, goes back to a *Hortus medicus*. The garden was moved to its present position in Inverleith in 1820.

Robert Graham, the director of the botanic garden, opened the first palm house in 1834. This was a building with an octagonal groundplan with a diameter of approximately 20 m and a height of approximately 14 m. The originally conical glass roof had wooden rafters.

Twenty years later some of the palms had become so tall that a new house was needed. Two Malay palms, a wine and a sago palm, had already pierced the roof with their leaves.

Professor Bailey Balfour commissioned a new building, and this was approved by Parliament in 1855. A photograph taken by Dr. James Duncan, which showed the old building with the palms growing out of the roof, was no doubt an irrefutable argument in favour of a new building. This was designed by Matheson, and building was begun in 1856 and finished two years later. It was constructed against the west side of the old palm house, so that the two became a unit.

The palm house was built of local sandstone with a roof of curved double-T supports which were reinforced lengthwise. The cross-section of the roof is the same as that of the palm house at Kew.

The unusual height of almost 22 m (the palm house at Kew is approximately 20 m in height) in relation to its area makes the building look badly proportioned. The massive sandstone facade simply strengthens the impression of excessive height. The head gardener, McNab, had pleaded for stone walls, since he believed that they would give the building better insulation and provide the necessary shade for certain species of palms. The building does not face south but west, since the detrimental effect of the sun on the plants was overestimated at the time. It is hard to understand today how, given the Scottish climate, there could have been apprehension about the exposure of the plants to the sun.

It took eight months to move the palms into the new building, since some had rootballs weighing several tons.

The *Falkirk Herald* reported on the new palm house on August 19 1858: 'They [the palms] seem thoroughly at home however, in their new place, and, lofty although the house be, if they proceed at their present rate of growth, few years will have elapsed before they be demanding more head room. The tropical aspect of this house is heightened by the fact that the man in attendance upon the visitors is a bona fide African. The presence of such a man gives consistency to the scene; and besides it is found that a native of the sunny climes, where the palm trees grow, is better able to stand the high temperature of such a house than one of our pale-faced race.'[81]

The roof of the old palm house was replaced with an iron structure in 1859. Later a glass wall was built between the old and the new building.

1, 2 Groundplan and elevation of the original buildings. On the right is the tropical palm house of 1834, on the left the temperate palm house of 1858. The conical roof of the tropical palm house was later replaced by a dome.

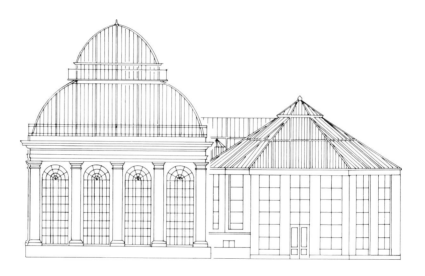

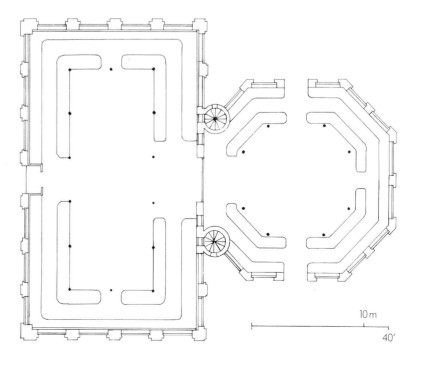

10 m

40'

3 The glass dome of the tropical palm house from the lower gallery of the temperate palm house.
4 View of the temperate palm house. The tropical palm house is behind on the right.

Kew (England), Royal Botanic Gardens, Temperate House (1860–99)
Design: Decimus Burton

This second large glasshouse complex at Kew was begun in 1860 at the urgent request of Sir William Hooker, after the collection of Chilean, Mexican, Australian and other plants from temperate zones had begun to sustain damage from years of makeshift accommodation. This time Decimus Burton supplied the designs without Turner's collaboration. The building firm of W. Cubitt & Co. put in the lowest tender and received the order.

The central building which is approximately 65 m long, and the two adjoining octagonal pavilions were finished in 1862. The cost had risen to £29,000, and building was delayed for thirty years until the construction of the outer wings was at last begun in 1894 at the instigation of Joseph Chambers, Secretary of State for the Colonies. The new building is even larger than the Palm House of 1844, covering an area of almost 4400 square metres. This is twice the size of the Palm House and three times the size of Paxton's Conservatory at Chatsworth.

The building was originally glazed in more than 6000 square metres of green glass. The roof was shaped like a tent since the straight surfaces made it possible to open parts of it for some months of the year. Cubitt's engineer developed a device by which the panes of glass of the three upper sections of the roof could be let down to lie on the glass further down. The rack and pinion mechanism was set in motion from the gallery.

As in the Palm House, the cast-iron columns served to drain the rainwater. The green glass was later replaced by clear glass, since the plants were not getting enough light.

Restoration of the whole complex was begun in 1978.

1 View of the central building from the east. The photograph was taken in 1978 at the beginning of the restoration.
2 Groundplan with plan of the roof.

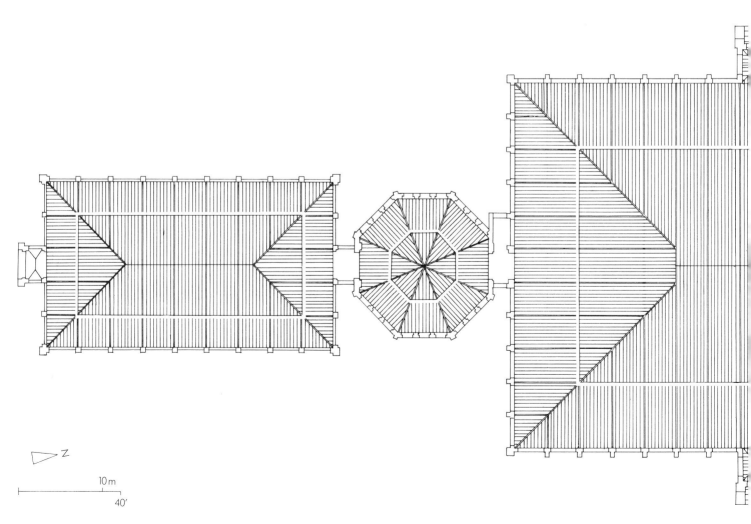

10 m

40'

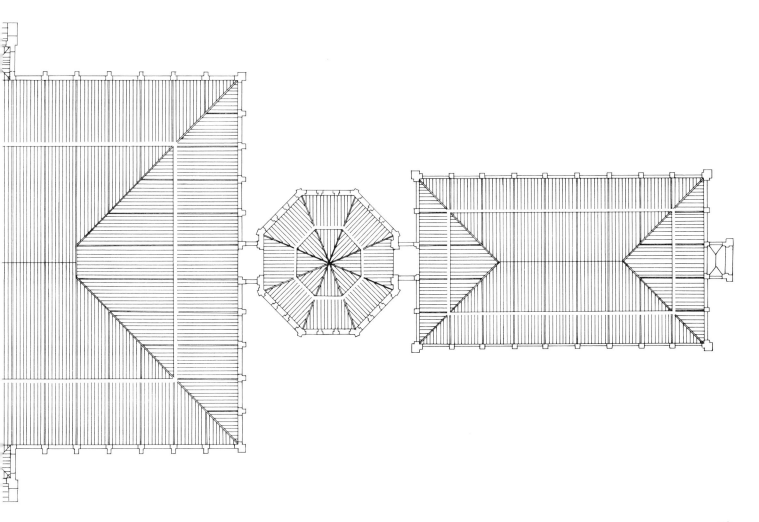

3 View of the northernmost pavilion.
4 View of one of the octagonal pavilions.
5 View of the highly decorated main entrance.
6 Detail of the rack and pinions for opening the
   upper windows of the side pavilions.

Glasgow (Scotland), Botanic Gardens, Kibble Palace (1865/73)
Design: John Kibble

The Glasgow Botanic Gardens were founded in 1817. One of its directors was the well-known botanist William Hooker who later became the director of the Royal Botanic Gardens at Kew. After Hooker left Glasgow in 1841, the botanic gardens were moved to Kelvinside where they are today.

The Botanic Gardens were at first only open to paying members of the Royal Botanic Society. The general public was only allowed in on Saturdays for an entrance fee of one shilling. On certain days the gardens were open to the 'working classes' at an entrance fee of one penny.

The large glasshouse originally belonged to John Kibble, the son of a wealthy Glasgow merchant.

When Kibble retired from business in 1865 he had the conservatory built on his property at Coulport, on Loch Long. He designed the glasshouse himself.

John Kibble was very versatile and was able, because of his wealth, to follow many different interests. He was an engineer but also a botanist and a photographer. He invented a huge camera which could take photographs that measured 90 x 110 cm. It was so heavy that it had to be put on a wheeled base and pulled by horses. He received a gold medal for his photography at the International Exhibition of 1851.

It was therefore not surprising that Kibble designed his own conservatory which was described in a contemporary daily paper as follows: 'Leaving this appartment we enter the great circular area, which most fitly completes the picture. The over arching glass dome is supported by 12 columns, and rests on a circular basement of fretwork finished in the Moorish style, and the whole interior is done up in white and gold. Here we have a third circular fountain, in the centre of which is a romantic looking island, studded with rocks and models of the most famous ruins in Greece and Rome. Two or three model ships are riding quietly at anchor in the island-harbours, and a tug steamer, about 15'' in length, with machinery and everything complete, may be seen hauling a vessel round the circle or into port as the case may be. Around the walls are fifty lifesize statues after the greatest masters, such as the Laocoon, the Apollo Belvedere, Diana, Perseus with the head of Medusa, the Venus de Medici, the Greek Slave, Gibson's tinted Venus, Thorvaldsen's Eve, Canova's Three Graces, Andromeda etc. etc., standing lifesize or in gigantic proportions amid shrubs and flowers from every part of the globe.'[82]

'Kibble Palace' was moved to the Botanic Gardens after Kibble had reached an agreement with the Botanic Society which gave him the right to hold concerts and other performances in his building for the next twenty-one years.

Kibble agreed to enlarge the building considerably. The 'Crystal Art Palace' was opened in 1873. The parts of the original conservatory were transported to Glasgow on a raft and given two new wings which opened out to the left and right of the entrance to the smaller domed hall. The diameter of the main dome was enlarged to almost 44 m, so that Disraeli was able to give his inaugural speech as Rector of the University there before an audience of 4000.

In the following years Kibble arranged lectures and concerts in his Art Palace for the Glasgow middle classes, for whom this building had a great attraction. Thanks to a grant from the city of Glasgow, the Botanic Gardens were able in 1881 to buy Kibble out, and to transform the Crystal Art Palace into a wintergarden. Many of the tree-ferns planted at the time can still be seen there.

In 1887 the Botanic Gardens came into the possession of the city of Glasgow and became a public park.

The original underfloor heating, covered with cast-iron gratings somewhat like those one can still see at Kew, was replaced by a new heating system in 1881. The main dome was originally covered in coloured glass, either wholly or in part, and some pink and light green panes of glass still remain.

1 Front view. Ventilation flaps lie under the base of the roof, and there is ventilation in the lantern-like structure on the roof-ridge.

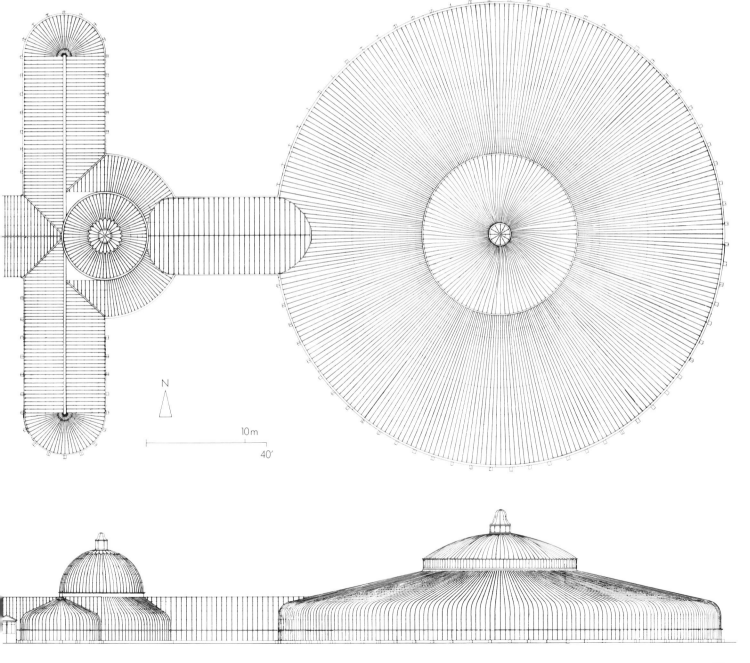

, 3 Plan of the roof and elevation.

N

10 m

40′

4 Side view of the great dome.

6 View of the small dome at the front.
7 Detail of a cast-iron column and bracket in the large dome.
8 Building parts like these cast-iron columns were prefabricated and available in any size. The Kibble Palace columns may have come from the wide range offered by MacFarlane's, the Glasgow manufacturers.

Laeken (Belgium), Royal Glasshouses (1865–99)

Design: Balat and Maquet

The Royal Glasshouses in the park of Laeken Palace on the outskirts of Brussels form a huge complex of glass buildings stretching over an area 600 m long and 200 m wide. Since the various glasshouses and conservatories are connected by glass-covered galleries, one can walk for more than half a mile without once going out into the open.

Differences in the level of the ground make it impossible to have a complete view of all the building, and it is difficult to orientate oneself in the interior of the labyrinthine complex.

If one begins a tour in the orangery, which is the only building dating back to 1865, the first building one comes to is a huge circular building which was used by Leopold II for court entertainments. Continuing straight on, rather than turning into the camellia house, one reaches the Congo House which was probably built to commemorate the founding of the Congo Free State. A white stone staircase leads from there to the *embarcadère*, the landing stage, a room decorated with statues and vases. The next large glasshouse is the House of Diana which lies on a hill, but first one passes through a glass-covered subterranean corridor which ends in a tunnel, its back wall covered in mirrors, so that the passage appears in duplicate. To the right of the mirror a staircase ascends to the surface and into the Pavilion of Narcissus, and from there through an 80 m long gallery climbing steeply to the House of Diana. Next comes a rhododendron house, a group of smaller glasshouses, and some buildings which are not open to the public and which all lie on the hill above the rotunda. Among them there is a large palm house

and the *Eglise de fer*, the iron church which is also a glass building in which church services were held among the tropical vegetation. The church has now been turned into a swimming bath.

Leopold II commissioned the complex when he succeeded his father on the throne in 1865 after travelling for some years through India, China, Egypt and North Africa. It was through his initiative that the Congo Free State was founded. This state, despite its name, was the king's private enterprise which brought him enormous wealth. Leopold's private dealings were criticised for years, until the Belgian state finally annexed Leopold's African possessions in 1908 and made them into the colony of the Belgian Congo. Without the king's great wealth which had come from the exploitation of the Congo, this complex would not have been built. The royal glasshouses represent an impressive testimonial to colonialism.

The outstanding building in the complex is the wintergarden which was designed by Auguste Balat (1818–1905) and built in 1876. Balat, who was Victor Horta's teacher, was the Belgian state architect. He designed the *Palais des Beaux-Arts* as well as many of the classical administrative buildings in the Belgian capital. A small waterplant house which he designed is today in the botanic garden at Meise (pages 60–1).

The wintergarden is a huge circular building 60 m in diameter and 30 m high. The iron framework of the dome rests on a sandstone ring supported by columns in the Tuscan style. Beyond this ring, the curved glass roof rises from a low plinth as far as the base of the dome. The roof is suspended from exterior ornamental iron ribs whose upper section runs in a continuous line to the skylight. Above the perpendicular windows of the tambour these ribs run beneath the glass

skin, and they are gathered into a twelve-sided ring below the skylight.

The two minarets which stand in front of the rotunda are the chimneys of the heating system, disguised as in the campanile at Kew (page 68). The desire to disguise industrial buildings went so far in the nineteenth century, that Sir Robert Rawlinson published a book in 1862 containing nothing but designs for a large variety of different disguises for industrial chimneys.[83]

Nothing was allowed to disturb the exotic illusion, which was a 'recompense for the demands of reality' for Leopold.[84] He died in one of his glasshouses in 1909.

The Royal Glasshouses are only open to the public in May.

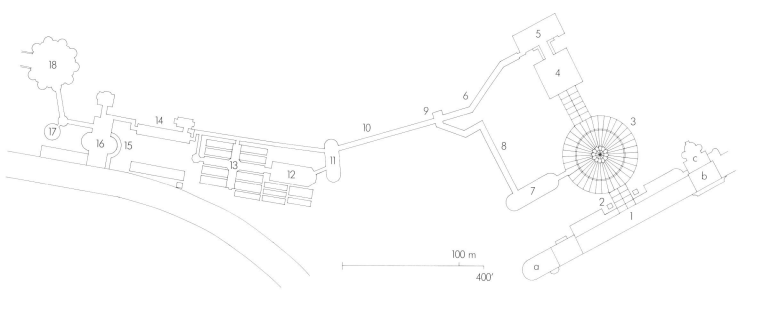

1 Plan: (1) Orangery and (a) diningroom, (b) theatre and (c) glasshouse, (2) minarets, (3) wintergarden and connecting buildings (1876), (4) Congo House (1886), (5) white staircase and *embarcadère,* (6) glass-covered subterranean corridor, (7) camellia house, (8) connecting gallery, (9) Pavilion of Narcissus, (10) ascending gallery, (11) House of Diana (1886), (12) rhododendron house, (13) group of small glasshouses, (14) azalea house, (15) rotunda, (16) palm house (1885), (17) sacristy, (18) iron and glass church used as a swimming bath today.

2 View of the wintergarden. On the right is the camellia house, on the left the Congo House. From the Congo House the white staircase leads down to the *embarcadère.*

7 View of the wintergarden.
8 View along the white staircase towards the *embarcadère*.
9 From here one reaches the open air when one leaves the *embarcadère*. In front of the exit stands a copy of Donatello's David.
10 Interior of the *embarcadère*.
11 From the *embarcadère* a subterranean corridor leads to the Pavilion of Narcissus.
12 On the right, the Pavilion of Narcissus. From here a staircase with a glass roof leads up to other buildings, the House of Diana, the palm house and the iron and glass church. The corridor to the left leads back to the camellia house.
13 The staircase with a glass roof.

8

11

9

12

10

13

14 The interior of the House of Diana.
15 The palm house and rotunda.

San Francisco (USA), Golden Gate Park, Palm House (1876–9)
Designer unknown

The palm house in the Golden Gate Park is one of two glasshouses that James Lick, a man of some substance, had ordered for his property at San Jose.

The buildings were brought round Cape Horn to San Francisco on a sailing ship specially chartered by James Lick.

The prefabricated building parts were still packed in boxes when Lick died in October 1876. The Society of California Pioneers inherited the two buildings and sold them for $2600 to a group of wealthy citizens who offered to present them to the park administration.

The only condition of the gift was that both conservatories should be erected within eighteen months.

The firm of Lord & Burnham of Irvington, New York, was commissioned to put up the structures. This was probably why Lord & Burnham were thought for many years to have been the manufacturers of the glass-houses. But it is evident from an exchange of letters between the donor and the park administration that both buildings had come from England, though it is not known which English manufacturer had been responsible for them.

Since the goldrush of 1849 when the city suddenly grew tremendously, it had become quite usual to import prefabricated buildings from England. Cast-iron and corrugated iron warehouses and stores were taken to pieces and shipped to San Francisco.

The palm house on the other hand is not made of cast-iron as might be expected, but of wood. Only the columns are of iron. Manufacturers like Cranston's in Birmingham, or Woodward and Lord & Burnham on the east coast of the United States used mostly wood which was thought to be preferable since it did not conduct heat and did not expand. An obvious disadvantage was the fact that building parts, especially decorated and openwork parts, could not be manufactured as efficiently in wood as in cast-iron.

The building was finished in 1879. F.A.Lord of Lord & Burnham had himself come from New York to oversee the work.

The central dome was almost completely destroyed by fire in 1883, but was rebuilt according to the original plans in the following year.

The earthquake of 1906 caused hardly any damage. Only some of the glass was broken.

It is not known what became of the second glasshouse. It may have been one of several forcing houses which no longer exist.

The building, classified as a historical monument, is listed today as 'California Historical Landmark No. 841'.

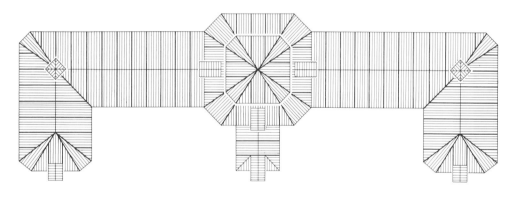

1 Plan of roof.
2 General view. At the beginning of the summer the glass panes are whitewashed against the strong sunlight.
3 View of the wooden structure of the central dome.
4 View of the central building.

Liverpool (England), Sefton Park, Palm House (1896)
Design: Mackenzie & Moncur

Sefton Park, the largest public park in Liverpool, was opened in 1872. The palm house was given to the city by Henry Yates Thompson, the son of a wealthy banker.

Thompson expressed the wish that the building was to be not only a wintergarden but a 'kind of Valhalla'. He commissioned various sculptors to produce statues of famous gardeners, botanists and explorers such as Le Nôtre, Linné, Captain Cook and Columbus.

The building, which was made of cast-iron, steel and glass, stands on a red granite plinth and is more than 20 m high. It was built by Mackenzie & Moncur of Edinburgh. This firm, founded in 1869, specialised in glasshouses and the installation of central heating systems. Old catalogues of Mackenzie & Moncur contain illustrations of public and private glasshouses and conservatories for botanic gardens and private clients, mostly titled, whose names are listed in an appendix to the catalogue.

Mackenzie & Moncur were also responsible for the two outer wings of Burton's Temperate House at Kew.

When the demand for large private glasshouses decreased after the First World War, the firm, which still exists today, began to specialise in heating and electrical installations.

The interior of the palm house, with its exotic plants and white marble sculptures, remains unchanged, and is a good example of the taste and aspirations of the close of the century. The statues of the great explorers represent the love of travel of the people of the port of Liverpool.

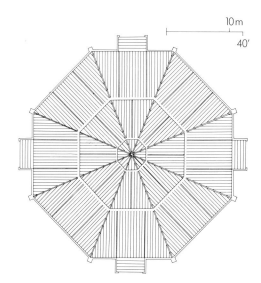

1 Plan of the roof.
2 View with statues by the sculptor Leon-Joseph Chavillaud: left Darwin, right Linné.

3 View of the structure of the roof.

104

7 On the gallery.
8 View of the gallery and spiral staircase.

New York (USA), The Bronx, New York Botanical Garden, Conservatory (1899–1902)
Design: William R. Cobb

The Botanical Garden of New York in the Bronx was founded in 1891 to be 'an American Kew'.

In a catalogue published at the time by the builders Lord & Burnham, the New York complex appears as a particularly impressive example of the type of glasshouse this company built all over the United States.

The design of the building is attributed to the architect William R. Cobb. The vaulted glass roofs were modelled on English examples, but the vertical outer walls are richly decorated in the style of the Beaux-Arts classicism which was current in the nineties. Like the buildings on which it is modelled, the front is made up of a central building, side wings and corner pavilions, but other pavilions are attached at the back, so that the groundplan is in the form of a 'C'.

The building has been much altered during two modernisations, in 1938 and 1953. Many of the ornaments were removed, and later the classical entrance buildings to the palm house were demolished.

The architect Edward Larrabee Barnes recently began to restore the building with great care. This was made possible by a generous private donation, and the glasshouses are now once again more or less in their original condition.

The anterooms which were originally of cast-iron were reconstructed with the help of old photographs and incomplete plans, and copied in cast aluminium.

The iron structure with its roof ribs of wood and iron was carefully restored. Fortunately the short-cut to the problems of restoration, which would have been to replace the old ribs by stronger – and therefore larger – aluminium ribs, was rejected.

1 Aerial view.

2 View of the structure of the roof of the palm house.
3 View of the palm house and its side wings.
4 One of the anterooms of the palm house (page 108).
5 Interior of the east pavilion (page 109).

Notes

1 (John Claudius Loudon), *The Greenhouse Companion,* London, 1824, p. 3.

2 William Marlin, 'Excellence attracts excellence. Kevin Roche, John Dinkeloo & Associates design a new building for Deere & Company, reaping a powerful precedent', *Architectural Record,* 1979, no. 2, pp. 85–92.

3 John Claudius Loudon, *Encyclopaedia of Gardening,* London, 1822, p. 926.

4 *Handbuch der Architektur,* IV, 6, 4, Stuttgart, 1906, p. 489.

5 John Claudius Loudon, *Encyclopaedia of Gardening,* London, 1822, p. 342.

6 *Handbuch der Architektur,* IV, 6, 4, loc. cit., p. 489.

7 Cf.: Arnold Tschira, *Orangerien und Gewächshäuser,* dissertation, Berlin, 1939, p. 14.

8 Denis Diderot and Jean-Baptiste d'Alembert (eds.), *Encyclopédie ou dictionnaire raisonné des sciences, des arts et des métiers,* Paris, 1751–77, vol. XV, 116 b.

9 Cf.: Arnold Tschira, *Orangerien und Gewächshäuser,* loc. cit., p. 69.

10 The garden of the Hesperides is a garden in Greek mythology which is guarded by the four Hesperides, the goddesses of the night. Christoph Volkamer named his books, which appeared in 1708 and 1714 in Nuremberg, after this garden. See also: Arnold Tschira, *Orangerien und Gewächshäuser,* loc. cit., pp. 16 ff., pp. 76 ff.

11 John Claudius Loudon, *Remarks on the Construction of Hothouses,* London, 1817, p. 47.

12 Denis Diderot and Jean-Baptiste d'Alembert (eds.), *Encyclopédie...,* loc. cit., vol. XV, 116 b. (Further articles about glasshouses: vol. XVII, 156 b; vol. I, 627 b; vol. XVII, 27 b. Illustrations in the book of plates no. I under 'Jardinage'.)

13 John Claudius Loudon, *Encyclopaedia of Gardening,* London, 1878, p. 158.

14 Ibid., p. 159.

15 Ibid., p. 279.

16 Quoted from: Charles MacIntosh, *The Greenhouse, Hothouse and Stove,* London, 1838, p. 361.

17 Ibid., p. 362.

18 John Claudius Loudon, *An Encyclopaedia of Cottage, Farm and Villa Architecture and Furniture,* London, 1833, p. 979 f.

19 Charles MacIntosh, *The Greenhouse, Hothouse and Stove,* loc. cit., p. 6.

20 John Claudius Loudon, *Remarks on the Construction of Hothouses,* loc. cit., p. 49.

21 John Claudius Loudon, *Encyclopaedia of Gardening,* London, 1878, p. 586.

22 Cf.: John Gloag, *Mr. Loudon's England,* London, 1970, pp. 45 f.

23 Cf.: John Claudius Loudon, *Encyclopaedia of Gardening,* London, 1878, p. 585.

24 Cf.: Arnold Tschira, *Orangerien und Gewächshäuser,* loc. cit., pp. 17, 81.

25 John Claudius Loudon, *An Encyclopaedia of Cottage, Farm and Villa Architecture and Furniture,* London, 1853, p. 980.

26 Ibid., pp. 1112 ff., 1124.

27 Quoted from: *The Builder* (London), 1848, p. 515.

28 John Claudius Loudon, *Encyclopaedia of Gardening,* London, 1822, p. 927.

29 Exhaustive information on this subject can be found in: Gilbert Herbert, *Pioneers of Prefabrication,* London and Baltimore, 1978.

30 Ibid., p. 176.

31 John Claudius Loudon, *Encyclopaedia of Gardening,* London, 1878, p. 1212.

32 Ibid., p. 122 f.

33 Ibid., p. 1214 f.

34 Quoted from: John Claudius Loudon, *Encyclopaedia of Gardening,* London, 1878, p. 94.

35 Cf.: Henry-Russell Hitchcock, *Architecture: Nineteenth and Twentieth Centuries,* Harmondsworth, 1971, p. 172.

36 *Moniteur des architectes* (Paris), 1860, vol. 58, plates 694–696.

37 Cf.: *Les Monuments historiques de la France* (Paris), 1979, April, pp. 10 ff.; *Hector Horeau, 1801–1872,* exhibition catalogue, Centre d'Etudes et de Recherches Architecturales, Paris, n. d.

38 H. Jäger, *Gartenkunst und Gärten, sonst und jetzt,* Berlin, 1888, p. 516.

39 *Berlin und seine Bauten,* Berlin, 1896, vol. 2, p. 254.

40 Paul Ortwin Rave, *Karl Friedrich Schinkel. Berlin III,* Berlin, 1962, pp. 77–81.

41 Cf.: *Zeitschrift für Praktische Baukunst* (Berlin), 1863, pp. 241 ff.

42 Cf.: *Zeitschrift für Bauwesen* (Berlin), 1887, p. 69.

43 Cf.: Henry-Russell Hitchcock, *Architecture: Nineteenth and Twentieth Centuries,* loc. cit., p. 188.

44 Cf.: Klaus Döhmer, *'In welchem Style sollen wir bauen?',* Munich, 1976, p. 112.

45 Title of a treatise published in 1828 by Heinrich Hübsch.

46 Klaus Döhmer, *'In welchem Style sollen wir bauen?',* loc. cit., pp. 119 ff.

47 John Claudius Loudon, *Encyclopaedia of Gardening,* London, 1878, p. 1023.

48 Ibid., p. 585.

49 Ibid., p. 1023.

50 (John Claudius Loudon), *The Greenhouse Companion,* loc. cit., pp. 14 f.

51 Cf.: *Historismus und Bildende Kunst.* Lectures by Pevsner, Grote, Evers and others, Munich, 1965.

52 Heinrich Kreisel, *Die Schlösser Ludwigs II. in Bayern,* Darmstadt, 1963, p. 24.

53 H. Jäger, *Gartenkunst und Gärten, sonst und jetzt,* loc. cit., p. 516.

54 John Claudius Loudon, *Encyclopaedia of Gardening,* London, 1878, p. 278.

55 M. Neumann, *Grundsätze und Erfahrungen über die Anlage, Erhaltung und Pflege von Glashäusern aller Art,* Weimar, 1852, pp. 68 f.

56 John Claudius Loudon, *Encyclopaedia of Gardening,* London, 1878, p. 194.

57 Walter Benjamin, *Paris, die Hauptstadt des XIX. Jahrhunderts,* in: *Illuminationen,* Frankfurt, 1969, p. 188.

58 Walter Imhoof, *Der 'Europamüde' in der deutschen Erzählliteratur,* Leipzig, 1930.

59 Walter Benjamin, *Paris, die Hauptstadt des XIX. Jahrhunderts,* loc. cit., p. 193.

60 Guy de Maupassant, *Bel Ami,* Paris (Albin Michel), p. 379.

61 The author of these articles was César Daly.

62 *The Builder* (London), 1895, pp. 144 f.

63 Haus-Rucker-Co., *Rooftop Oasis Project,* New York, 1976 (published privately).

64 Cf.: *Les Monuments historiques de la France* (Paris), 1978, no. 1, pp. 5, 6.

65 Cf.: *Wiener Bauindustriezeitung* (Vienna), 1887, p. 462.

66 Cf.: *Allgemeine Bauzeitung* (Vienna), 1846, pp. 267–271, plates 54–56.

67 *Zeitschrift für Bauwesen* (Berlin), 1881, pp. 180 ff., plates 38–42.

68 Wolfgang Herrmann, *Deutsche Baukunst des XIX. und XX. Jahrhunderts,* Basel, 1977, part II, p. 50.

69 *The Building News* (London), 1876, p. 73.

70 *Deutsche Bauzeitung* (Berlin), 1873, p. 164.

71 *Handbuch der Architektur,* IV, 4, 1. Stuttgart, 1904, p. 225.

72 John Claudius Loudon, *Encyclopaedia of Gardening,* London, 1878, pp. 596, 597.

73 Cf.: Karl Paetow, *Klassizismus und Romantik auf Wilhelmshöhe,* Kassel, 1929, p. 56.

74 Quoted from: John Gloag, *Mr. Loudon's England,* loc. cit., p. 46.

75 Hix supposes that the building was erected after 1843. Cf.: John Hix, *The Glasshouse,* London, 1974, p. 27.

76 John Claudius Loudon, *An Encyclopaedia of Cottage, Farm and Villa Architecture and Furniture,* London, 1833, p. 980.

77 Cf.: Gilbert Herbert, *The Enigma of the Camellia House at Wollaton Hall,* unpublished manuscript, 1973.

78 Acarie-Baron, *Album du Jardin des Plantes de Paris,* Paris 1838, p. 11.

79 Ludwig von Zanth, *Die Wilhelma,* Stuttgart (?), 1855, preface.

80 Ibid.

81 Quoted from: Harold R. Fletcher and William H. Brown, *The Royal Botanic Garden Edinburgh 1670–1970,* Edinburgh, 1970, pp. 145 f.

82 Quoted from: Graham T. Smith, *The Kibble Palace,* dissertation, Glasgow, 1971.

83 Cf.: John Gloag, *Victorian Comfort. A Social History of Design from 1830–1900.* New York, 1973.

84 Liane Ramieri, *Léopold II., urbaniste,* Brussels, 1973.

Bibliography

Separate Publications

Acarie-Baron, Album du Jardin des Plantes de Paris, Paris, 1838.

Balfour, John Hutton, Guide to the Royal Botanic Garden Edinburgh, Edinburgh, 1873.

Baltrusaitis, Jurgis, Aberrations. Quatre essais sur la légende des formes, Paris, 1957.

Bean, W. J., The Royal Botanic Garden Kew, London, 1908.

Britz, Billie Sherryll, The Greenhouse at Lyndhurst, Washington, 1977.

Cario, Louis, and Charles Régismanset, L'Exotisme. La littérature coloniale, Paris, 1911.

Chadwick, G. F., The Works of Sir Joseph Paxton, London, 1961.

Chinard, Gilbert, L'Amérique et le rêve exotique dans la littérature française au XVIIe et au XVIIIe siècle, Paris, 1913.

Clément, Jules, Alphonse Balat, architecte du roi, Brussels, 1956.

Derreth, Otto, Gärten im alten Frankfurt, Frankfurt, 1976.

Döhmer, Klaus, 'In welchem Style sollen wir bauen?', Munich, 1976.

Fischer, Wend, Geborgenheit und Freiheit. Vom Bauen mit Glas, Krefeld, 1970.

Fletcher, Harold R., and William H. Brown, The Royal Botanic Garden Edinburgh 1670–1970, Edinburgh, 1970.

Gloag, John, Victorian Taste. Some Social Aspects of Architecture and Industrial Design from 1820–1900, New York, 1962.

Gloag, John, Mr. Loudon's England, London, 1970.

Gloag, John, Victorian Comfort. A Social History of Design from 1830–1900, New York, 1973.

Handbuch der Architektur, IV, 4, 1, 'Wirtschaften, Vergnügungsstätten, Gasthöfe', Stuttgart, 1904.

Handbuch der Architektur, IV, 6, 4, 'Gebäude für Sammlungen und Ausstellungen', Stuttgart, 1906.

Heidelbach, Paul, Geschichte der Wilhelmshöhe, Leipzig, 1909.

Hennig-Schoefeld, Monica, and Helga Schmidt-Thomsen, Transparenz und Masse, Köln, 1972.

Henschel commemorative publication, Kassel, 1900.

125 Jahre Henschel 1810–1935, Kassel, 1935.

Herbert, Gilbert, The Enigma of the Camellia House at Wollaton Hall, unpublished manuscript, 1973.

Herbert, Gilbert, Pioneers of Prefabrication, London and Baltimore, 1978.

Herrmann, Wolfgang, Deutsche Baukunst des XIX. und XX. Jahrhunderts, Basel, 1977.

Historismus und Bildende Kunst, Pevsner, Grote, Evers and others, Munich, 1965.

Hitchcock, Henry-Russell, Architecture Nineteenth and Twentieth Centuries, Harmondsworth, 1971.

Hitching's Greenhouses, ca. 1923.

Hix, John, The Glasshouse, London, 1974.

Hector Horeau, 1801–1872, exhibition catalogue, Centre d'Etudes et de Recherches Architecturales, Paris, n. d.

Hughes, Quentin, Seaport. Architecture and Townscape in Liverpool, London, 1964.

Jäger, H., Gartenkunst und Gärten, sonst und jetzt, Berlin, 1888.

Die Bau- und Kunstdenkmäler im Regierungsbezirk Kassel, vol. IV, Marburg, 1910.

Klingender, Francis D., Art and the Industrial Revolution, St. Albans, 1975.

Kreisel, Heinrich, Die Schlösser Ludwigs II. in Bayern, Darmstadt, 1963.

Lord & Burnham, Catalogue of Greenhouses, catalogue, ca. 1903.

Lord & Burnham, Glass Gardens as We Know Them, catalogue, ca. 1919–20.

Loudon, John Claudius, Remarks on the Construction of Hothouses, London, 1817.

Loudon, John Claudius, Encyclopaedia of Gardening, London, 1822.

Loudon, John Claudius, Encyclopaedia of Gardening, London, 1878 (revised edition).

(Loudon, John Claudius), The Greenhouse Companion, London, 1824.

Loudon, John Claudius, An Encyclopaedia of Cottage, Farm and Villa Architecture and Furniture, London, 1833.

Loudon, John Claudius, An Encyclopaedia of Cottage, Farm and Villa Architecture and Furniture, London, 1853.

Loudon, John Claudius (ed.), The Landscape Gardening of Sir Humphrey Repton, London, 1840.

MacFarlane, Walter, and Co., Illustrated Catalogue, catalogue, 1882/83.

McGrath, Raymond, and A. C. Frost, Glass in Architecture and Decoration, London, 1937.

MacIntosh, Charles, The Greenhouse, Hothouse and Stove, London, 1838.

Mackenzie & Moncur, catalogue, 1900.

Mackenzie & Moncur, Modern Glasshouses, catalogue.

Messenger & Co., Artistic Conservatories, catalogue, 1880.

Meyer, Alfred Gotthold, Eisenbauten. Ihre Geschichte und Ästhetik, Esslingen, 1907.

Meyer, Karl H., Königliche Gärten, Hanover, 1966.

Neumann, M., Grundsätze und Erfahrungen über die Anlage, Erhaltung und Pflege von Glashäusern aller Art, Weimar, 1852.

Paetow, Karl, Klassizismus und Romantik auf Wilhelmshöhe, Kassel, 1929.

Rave, Paul Ortwin, Karl Friedrich Schinkel. Berlin III, Berlin, 1962.

Rohault, Karl (Charles Rohault de Fleury), Das Naturhistorische Museum in Paris. Muséum d'Histoire Naturelle à Paris, Vienna, 1837.

Schild, Erich, Zwischen Glaspalast und Palais des Illusions, Frankfurt, 1967.

Schwarzer, Erwin, 'Johann Conrad Bromeis, Oberbaudirektor', in: Lebensbilder aus Kurhessen und Waldeck 1830–1930, Marburg, 1950.

Smith, Graham T., The Kibble Palace, dissertation, Glasgow, 1971.

Spiekermann, Heinz, Gußglas im Hochbau, Schorndorf, 1966.

Tschira, Arnold, Orangerien und Gewächshäuser, dissertation, Berlin, 1939.

Ward, Lock & Co., Syon House. Its Picture Galleries and Gardens, London, 1851.

Wendland, Folkwin, Berlins Gärten und Parke, Frankfurt, 1979.

Woodward, E. and F. W., Woodward's Graperies and Horticultural Buildings, New York, 1865.

Zanth, Ludwig von, Die Wilhelma, Stuttgart (?), 1855.

Articles in Periodicals

AR   Architectural Record, New York
ASB   Architektonisches Skizzenbuch, Berlin
ABZ   Allgemeine Bauzeitung, Vienna
B   The Builder, London
BN   The Building News (= The Freehold Land Times), London
CM   La Construction moderne, Paris
DB   Deutsche Bauzeitung (= Wochenblatt des Deutschen Architekten- und Ingenieurvereins, Berlin), Berlin
DIZ   Deutsche Illustrierte Zeitung, Berlin
GC   Le Génie civil, Paris
MA   Moniteur des architectes, Paris
MH   Les Monuments historiques de la France, Paris
NA   Nouvelles annales de la construction, Paris
RG   Révue générale de l'architecture, Paris
WBZ   Wiener Bauindustriezeitung, Vienna
ZBV   Zentralblatt der Bauverwaltung, Berlin
ZBH   Zeitschrift für Bauhandwerker (= Haarmann's Zeitschrift für Bauhandwerker), Brunswick
ZB   Zeitschrift für Bauwesen, Berlin
ZPB   Zeitschrift für Praktische Baukunst (= Romberg's Zeitschrift für Praktische Baukunst), Berlin
ZI   Zeitschrift des Vereins Deutscher Ingenieure, Berlin

Adams, Maurice B., 'Art in the Conservatory and Greenhouse', BN, 1880, pp. 64 f., 96 f., 100.

Aitchison, G., 'Conservatory in Cast and Wrought Iron, Chesham Place', B, 1895, pp. 144 f.

'Aquaria and Wintergardens', BN, 1876, vol. 30, pp. 109, 135, 188.

Auhagen, ' Über Palmenhäuser', DB, 1876, p. 438. ' The Duke of Connaught's Conservatory at Bagshot', B, 1880, p. 486.

'New Pavilion and Wintergarden, Blackpool', BN, 1878, vol. 35, 19 July.

Charpentier and Brousse, 'Jardin d'hiver . . . à St. Hilaire-St. Florent'. NA, 1880, p. 182, plates 54, 55.

'The Conservatory at Chatsworth', B, 1848, p. 515.

'Cheltenham, Wintergarden and Skating Rink', BN, 1876, vol. 31, p. 1, and 1887, vol. 52, p. 353.

Constantine, Eleni M., 'Restoring a Victorian botanical conservatory. New York Botanical Garden Conservatory', AR, 1980, no. 10, pp. 72–77.

Cranston, James, 'Horticultural Buildings', BN, 1863, p. 780.

'Der Winterpalast in Dublin', ABZ, 1866, 21 f., sheets 9, 10.

Eggert, H.: 'Kaiser Wilhelms-Universität Straßburg. Der Garten des Botanischen Instituts', ZB, 1888, pp. 199 ff., plates 30–33.

Ende: 'Anlage eines Gewächshauses in der Villa des Herrn Ravené in Berlin', ZPB, 1861, pp. 193 f., plates 21, 22.

Ende, Max am, 'Der Ausstellungspalast und Wintergarten zu Dublin', ZI, 1866, pp. 35, 711, plates 1, 22, 23, sheets 24–26.

Foucart, Bruno, 'Au plaisir des architectes. Les villes d'eau et leur architecture aux XIXe et XXe siècle', MH, 1978, no. 1, pp. 2 ff.

'Das Curhaus, Palmengarten und Sommertheater in der orthopädischen Anstalt in Göggingen bei Augsburg', WBZ, 1887, no. 38, pp. 461 f.

'Architekten- und Ingenieurverein zu Hannover (Erweiterung des Palmenhauses im Berggarten zu Hannover-Herrenhausen)', DB, 1879, p. 245.

Herter, 'Das neue Palmenhaus im Kgl. Botanischen Garten zu Schöneberg in Berlin', ZPB, 1863, pp. 241 ff.

Herter, 'Treibhaus der Villa Reichenheim bei Berlin', ASB, no. 24, sheet 3.

Hitzig, 'Treibhaus bei Berlin mit Gärtnerwohnung und herrschaftlichem Salon', ASB, no. 8, sheet 3.

Hude, von der, und Hennicke, 'Das Central Hotel in Berlin – II. Der Wintergarten', ZB, p. 180 ff., plates 38–42.

Hügelin, 'Serre, Boulevard Arago à Paris', CM, 1886/87, vol. 2, pp. 283, 294, plates 47–50.

Jeanson, 'Eisernes Gewächshaus zu St. Adresse . . .', ABZ, 1862, p. 242.

'The new Palm House, Kew Gardens', B, 1848, pp. 29 ff.

'The Temperate House, Royal Botanic Gardens, Kew', B, 1861, p. 23 ff.

'The New Temperate House in Kew Gardens', BN, 1897, vol. 72, p. 234, 273.

Körner et al., 'Der neue Botanische Garten in Dahlem bei Berlin', ZBV, 1897, p. 230–233.

'Die baulichen Anlagen des Botanischen Gartens zu Kopenhagen', DB, 1881, p. 133 ff., 145 ff.

'Krolls Garten', ABZ, 1846, vol. 11, pp. 267 ff., plates 54–56.

LeCoeur, 'Galerie-serre dans un hotel privé à Paris', RG, 1877, pp. 108 f., plates 28–30.

Loyer, François, 'La grande kermesse de Hector Horeau', MH, 1979, April, pp. 10 ff.

Monmory, F., 'Le Palais d'hiver au jardin d'acclimatation à Paris', GC, 1894, vol. 25, p. 257 ff., plate 17, and 1895, vol. 28, pp. 65 ff., plate 5.

'Jardin d'hiver à Paris, détruit', MA, 1860, vol. 58, plates 694–696.

'Le nouveau jardin fleuriste de la Ville de Paris', GC, 1898, vol. 33, pp. 229 ff., plate 15.

Persius, 'Orangeriehaus im Paulinenhof', ZPB, 1868, pp. 335 f., plate 37.

'Über das neue Palmenhaus im kaiserlichen botanischen Garten zu St. Petersburg', ZPB, 1850, pp. 91 ff., plate 19.

Rohault de Fleury, Charles, 'Gewächshäuser', ZPB, 1851, p. 327, plates 35–37.

Rohault de Fleury, Charles, RG, 1849, pp. 254 ff., plates 25, 36, 37.

Schinkel, Karl Friedrich, 'Treibhaus der Villa Gräfe in Tiergarten bei Berlin. Treibhaus des Herrn Geheimen Oberhofbuchdrucker Decker zu Berlin', ASB, no. 40, sheet 3.

'Das neue Palmenhaus in Schönbrunn', DIZ, 1887, no. 33, pp. 128 f.

Schulze, F., 'Gewächshaus-Anlagen in England, Belgien und Holland', ZB, 1887, pp. 67–82, plates 14, 15.

Segenschmied et al., 'Palmenhaus im Botanischen Garten des Kaiserl. Lustschlosses Schönbrunn', WBZ, 1898, no. 15, p. 38, plate 100.

Stier, Hubert, 'Berliner Neubauten. Die Flora zu Charlottenburg', DB, 1873, pp. 121 ff, 125, 149 ff., 163 ff., 171 f., 175, 259 f., 269 ff.

'The Tynemouth Aquarium and Wintergarden', BN, 1876, vol. 30, p. 60.

Voit, August von, 'Die Neubauten im Kgl. Botanischen Garten zu München', ZB, 1867, pp. 315–324, plates 34–39.

Voyant, 'Petit jardin d'hiver à Paris, rue d'Offément', NA, 1879, p. 73, plate 26.

'The Royal Aquarium, Westminster', BN, 1876, vol. 30, pp. 73 f.

Wiebenson, Dora, 'Le Parc Monceau et ses "Fabriques"', MH, 1976 no. 5, pp. 16 ff.

'Beschreibung des großen Gewächshauses im botanischen Garten der königlichen Universität zu Würzburg', ABZ, 1860, pp. 27, 29 ff., plate 321.

Acknowledgements

Art Nouveau Belgium/France, Houston, 1976: 42 centre

Bayerische Verwaltung der Staatlichen Schlösser, Gärten und Seen, Munich (photographer: Joseph Albert): 39

Verwaltung der Staatlichen Schlösser und Gärten Berlin: 37

The Building News, 1863: 26 bottom

The Chatsworth Trustees: 23

The Civil Engineer and Architect's Journal, 1850: 24 top

Deutsche Bauzeitung, 1873: 46

Deutsche Illustrierte Zeitung, 1887: 33

Deutsches Museum, Munich: 26 top

Denis Diderot and Jean-Baptiste d'Alembert (eds.), Encyclopédie ou dictionnaire raisonné des sciences, des arts et des métiers, Paris, 1751–77: 11

Wend Fischer, Geborgenheit und Freiheit. Vom Bauen mit Glas, Krefeld, 1970: 32

Historisches Museum Frankfurt: 46 top

Handbuch der Architektur, IV, 4, 1, Stuttgart 1904: 47 top

Handbuch der Architektur, IV, 6, 4, Stuttgart 1906: 43, 45 bottom

Haus-Rucker-Co.: 8

Stadtarchiv Kassel: 13 top

John Claudius Loudon, Encyclopaedia of Gardening, London, 1822: 19 (1–4), 24 bottom

(John Claudius Loudon), The Greenhouse Companion, London, 1824: 36

John Claudius Loudon, An Encyclopaedia of Cottage, Farm and Villa Architecture and Furniture, London, 1833: 17, 21 bottom

John Claudius Loudon, Encyclopaedia of Gardening, London, 1878: 10, 29, 30, 31, 53 top

Walter MacFarlane and Co., Illustrated Catalogue, 1882/3: 27

Mackenzie & Moncur, Modern Glasshouses: 45 top

Messenger & Co., Artistic Conservatories, 1880: 44

M. Neumann, Grundsätze und Erfahrungen über die Anlage, Erhaltung und Pflege von Glashäusern aller Art, Weimar, 1852: 20 bottom, 22, 62 top

Karl Rohault (Charles Rohault de Fleury), Das Naturhistorische Museum in Paris, Muséum d'Histoire Naturelle à Paris, Wien, 1837: 19 bottom, 20 top, 28, 62 bottom

Graham T. Smith: 83

Franz Stoedtner, Düsseldorf: 41

Alexandra Timchula, New York: 106

Arnold Tschira, Orangerien und Gewächshäuser, Berlin, 1939: 13 bottom

Zeitschrift für Bauwesen, 1867: 34 bottom

Zeitschrift für Bauwesen, 1888: 34 top

The illustrations on pages 24 top, 29 bottom, 30 and 31 have been placed at our disposal by the Royal Institute of British Architects (RIBA), the illustration on page 26 bottom by the British Library.

All photographs that are not mentioned here have been taken by the author.